Get
healthy
for good

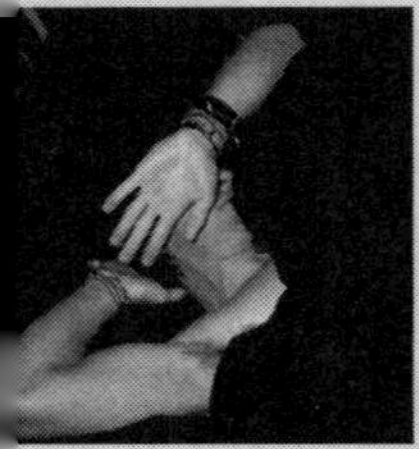
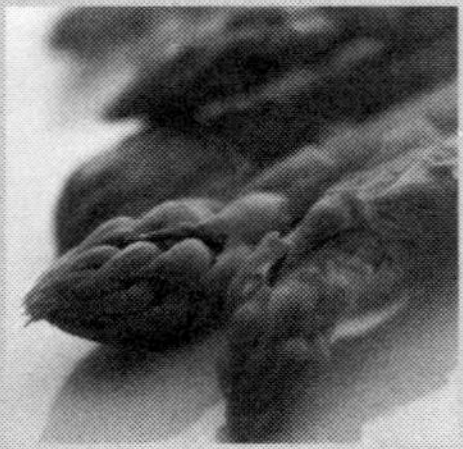
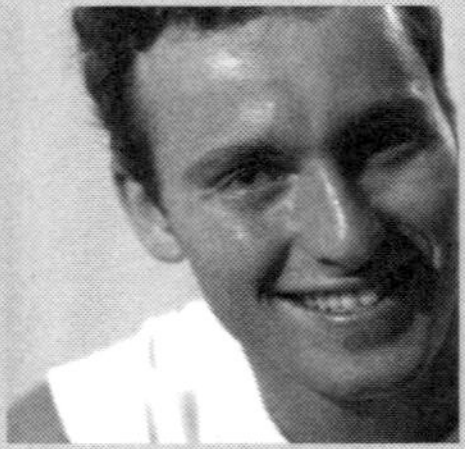
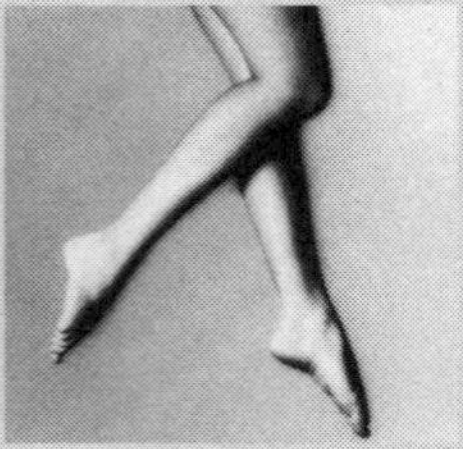
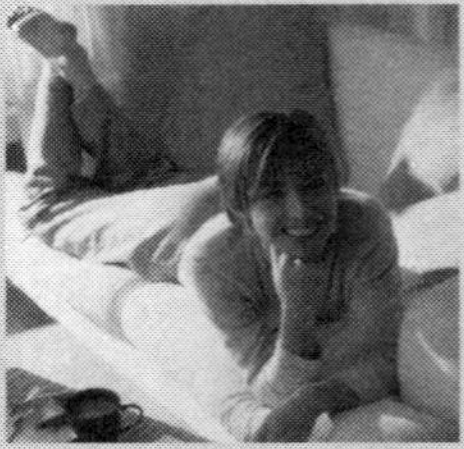

Get healthy for good

52 brilliant ideas for mind and body well-being

Kate Cook

brilliantideas

Careful now
It's your life so be sensible about how you take care of it. You should consult your doctor or healthcare provider before changing your diet, undergoing any kind of change to your exercise routine or taking any nutritional supplements.

If you have any health problems of any nature – physical, emotional or mental – always consult the proper healthcare providers.

Although the contents of this book were checked at the time of going to press, the world keeps moving and the World Wide Web does so twice as fast. This means the publisher and author cannot guarantee the contents of any of the websites mentioned in the text.

The author and publisher would like to thank Steve Shipside for his contribution to this book. Steve is the author of *Win at the Gym* and *Power-up Pilates* in the 52 Brilliant Ideas series. Thanks also to Seki Tijani, who helped the author with her research.

Copyright © The Infinite Ideas Company Limited, 2005, 2007

The right of Kate Cook to be identified as the author of this book has been asserted in accordance with the Copyright, Designs and Patents Act 1988

First published in 2005 as Whole health
This edition published 2007 by
The Infinite Ideas Company Limited
36 St Giles
Oxford
OX1 3LD
United Kingdom
www.infideas.com

All rights reserved. Except for the quotation of small passages for the purposes of criticism and review, no part of this publication may be reproduced, stored in a retrieval system or transmitted in any form or by any means, electronic, mechanical, photocopying, recording, scanning or otherwise, except under the terms of the Copyright, Designs and Patents Act 1988 or under the terms of a licence issued by the Copyright Licensing Agency Ltd, 90 Tottenham Court Road, London W1T 4LP, UK, without the permission in writing of the publisher. Requests to the publisher should be addressed to the Permissions Department, Infinite Ideas Limited, 36 St Giles, Oxford, OX1 3LD, UK, or faxed to +44 (0)1865 514777.

A CIP catalogue record for this book is available from the British Library.

ISBN 978-1-905940-14-1

Brand and product names are trademarks or registered trademarks of their respective owners.

Designed and typeset by Baseline Arts Ltd, Oxford
Printed in India

Brilliant ideas

Brilliant features xiii

Introduction xiv

1. **What goes in must come out** 1
   Alimentary, my dear Watson. A quick tour of how your digestion works is a useful foundation to health, and a great ice-breaker at parties.

2. **Digestion up close and personal** 7
   An inefficient bowel is the genesis of several major degenerative diseases, including cancer. Good health starts with good digestion, so let's take a closer look at yours.

3. **Vital energy** 11
   We need an endless supply of energy to do everything we need and want to do in our lives, yet we're often overwhelmed by a desire to have a swift forty winks.

4. **Stressed out** 17
   You rarely realise how stressed you are till the day you chew the head off a shop assistant for taking too long at the till. However, when you do lose your cool like this, it's time to admit you've got a problem.

5. **What's in what?** 21
   Which foods should you target for good health? Here's a quick guide to what's in your food.

6. **Get organic** 25
   With more and more headlines screaming at us every day about unsafe food, is it any wonder that we're turning to organic food in our droves? But is it worth it?

7. **Superfoods** 29
   What exactly are superfoods? Comic-book heroes with a mission to save the world?

8. **Eat fat** 33
   Shops are full of low-fat everything, from cookies and cakes to yoghurt and tofu. In fact, the body desperately needs fats, but only the right kind will do.

9. **What's bothering you?** 37
   What do you think are the top three complaints dealt with in my clinic on a day-to-day basis?

10. **Skin from within** 41
    With great nutrition and a little care, you can achieve great-looking skin in no time at all.

11. **Water babies** 47
    Seventy per cent of the planet is covered in water, and when we're born 70% of us is water too. It's cool to be wet, so why aren't you drinking enough of the stuff?

12. **Allergy or intolerance?** 51
    Is it my imagination or is everyone suffering from allergies these days?

13. **Ready for a detox?** 55
    Detox is such a big buzz word these days, but what exactly does it mean?

14. **Chemical world** 59
    We can't avoid all the man-made chemicals out there. We can, however, choose alternatives for many.

15. **Getting into shape** 63
    Weight loss is for life and not just for after Christmas.

16. **Labelling matters** 67
    Have you ever looked at the back of a packet of food and wondered where the actual food was?

17. **Get your nutritional act together** 73
    You've made the brilliant decision to take your health and nutrition into your own hands. Now what?

18. **What does a day look like?** 77
    It's a wonder we eat anything at all considering the masses of conflicting information regarding food and diet. How can we come out of this mire of information with a sensible eating programme?

19. **Ageing gracefully** 81
    We live in a youth culture, but the oldies are fighting back!

20. **Nutrition: the basics** 85
    There are so many different diets and ways of eating that it's no wonder we're thoroughly confused. Here's a balanced view of the basics of good nutrition.

21. **Out there and doing it** 89
    I hate the gym. So, what are the alternatives?

22. **Have a heart (rate monitor)** 95
    Do you hate jogging/running? All that wobbly flesh jigging up and down?

23. **Gotta run** 99
   Run for your health, social life, waistline or sanity. There are as many reasons to run as there are runners and if you get out there and find your own perfect pace you'll never look back.

24. **Geeing up for the gym** 103
   However much you might hate the idea of the gym, it can prove to be extremely effective and convenient in terms of your fitness goals and it doesn't have to be boring.

25. **Stretching the point** 109
   Stretching is one of those things we know we should do, don't really know why and quietly forget about when no one's looking.

26. **The Hoover work-out** 113
   Why not make a real difference to your fitness by grabbing all the everyday opportunities?

27. **Take a walk on the wild side** 117
   Exercise doesn't have to involve sheathing yourself in Lycra and pounding mindlessly to hip-hop backbeats in front of banks of TV screens.

28. **Preposterous posture** 121
   Were you always nagged to sit up straight and stop slouching? If you didn't listen, chances are you're now suffering from an even bigger pain in the neck.

29. **Delegate your way to wellbeing** 125
   It's tempting to try and do everything perfectly. Unless you're superhuman, however, this could lead to one very tense life.

Brilliant ideas

30. **Human racing** 131
    Today many races are about comradeship, motivation, fun (yes, really) and perhaps the chance to do something for charity. Oh, and you get to bask in glory and show off your prize.

31. **Get on yer bike** 135
    It's difficult to injure yourself cycling because it's such a low-impact form of exercise, plus it's a great way to tone your legs and the nicest way to see the countryside.

32. **Yoga** 139
    Yoga is about being rather than doing. It's noncompetitive and a great balancer for the type of exercise you might do at the gym.

33. **Games other people play** 143
    If you left sports and team games behind with teenage crushes, acne and underage drinking, then perhaps you're missing out.

34. **Home spa** 147
    Why splash out on beauty treatments when you can achieve practically the same result in the comfort of your own home? Create your very own spa, take the phone off the hook, then lie back and enjoy.

35. **Kool kids kicking** 151
    How to get couch potatoes up off the couch and eating their greens.

36. **Let's face facts** 155
    Skin is your body's biggest organ. It mirrors your inner health and, unlike your other organs, the world gets to look at it.

37. **Dressing for success** 161
   What has dressing for success got to do with your whole health? Well, when you're confident and glowing this is a reflection of your state of health and mind.

38. **Design your life to work for you** 165
   Sometimes it's not the most talented, gifted or exceptional people that reach the top. So, what's stopping us?

39. **Effortless balance** 169
   If you feel you're working your life away, take stock of your life and do things differently.

40. **Clutter busting** 173
   Spare room full of dusty boxes and your cupboards stuffed with, well, stuff? Are there things lurking about in your loft that you don't want to know about?

41. **Soaring self-esteem** 177
   We formulate who we are through a lifetime of experience. As children, our self-confidence is either nurtured or destroyed depending on how we interpret events.

42. **Use your imagination** 181
   Consider this the instruction manual for the most powerful and underutilised tool you possess. Your brain.

43. **Working your purpose out** 187
   My particular purpose in life is lifting your game. What's yours?

44. **You're the most important person in your life** 191
   The worm has turned! Now it's time to put yourself first.

Brilliant ideas

45. **You have one day to live!** 195
    We undermine our health every day by not living in the present. Why spend all your time worrying about what might have been or what might happen tomorrow?

46. **Review of the greats** 199
    What can these old dogs teach us?

47. **Daily habits** 203
    It's the things that we do every day that kill us.

48. **Breathe in, breathe out!** 209
    Proper breathing can be a forgotten art for people in stressful jobs, lives or relationships. And these days we often hold onto our breath out of sheer terror.

49. **Space invaders** 213
    Find the space for your mind and meditate on a daily basis.

50. **Look on the bright side** 217
    It's time to reach for those rose-coloured spectacles...

51. **And so to bed...** 221
    It's two in the morning and you're still counting those blasted sheep. In fact, two million five hundred thousand have jumped over that gate so far!

52. **Retreat!** 227
    You've had enough! Life, work and the universe in general have become too much. You're having a 'Stop the world I want to get off' moment.

Bonus ideas 235

Brilliant resources 247

The End 249
Or is it a new beginning?

Where it's at 251
Index

Brilliant features

Each chapter of this book is designed to provide you with an inspirational idea that you can read quickly and put into practice straight away.

Throughout you'll find four features that will help you to get right to the heart of the idea:

- *Try another idea* If this idea looks like a life-changer then there's no time to lose. *Try another idea* will point you straight to a related tip to expand and enhance the first.

- *Here's an idea for you* Give it a go – right here, right now – and get an idea of how well you're doing so far.

- *Defining ideas* Words of wisdom from masters and mistresses of the art, plus some interesting hangers-on.

- *How did it go?* If at first you do succeed try to hide your amazement. If, on the other hand, you don't this is where you'll find a Q and A that highlights common problems and how to get over them.

Introduction

- Do you sleep badly because you fret about things?

- Do you worry that you don't eat as well as you should?

- Are you happy with your weight and complexion?

- Does stress threaten to swallow you up?

- Are you anxious about being unfit and unhealthy?

- Do you know where you're going in life?

Not so long ago people often talked about healthy lifestyles, an expression that still smacks of soap-powder people in white clothes with gleaming smiles on their way to play tennis, swim or kite surf. It seemed that a healthy lifestyle was all about losing weight, building muscle, doing everything in moderation and above all smiling smugly at everyone else in order to convince them of your superiority. This is all fine if that works for you, but what it doesn't really encompass is the idea that *real* health is a matter of mind as much as a matter of muscle. What *this* book is about is total wellbeing, inside and out, and as such it includes physical fitness, diet and nutrition and also the psychological side to all of these elements. This book is about the tricks that help you to keep going, eat better and most of all beat the stresses of modern life. I'm a life coach as well as a nutritionist, so the ideas in here aren't just about avoiding saturated fats, they're about helping you to identify and reach your goals. In the process you'll learn such things as why body image is so important.

This is a book for the modern age in which the demands of friends, family and careers threaten to swamp most of us. Yet the media never seems to run out of superpeople – supermodels, supermums, superstars – all of whom only seem to exist to show us up by deftly juggling jobs, families and fitness and sporting astonishing physiques. Nobody can promise to turn you into a superbreed, but with a bit of help you can learn to stop worrying about other people's definitions of success and focus a bit more on taking the time to take care of yourself.

By learning to appreciate yourself, take care of yourself and even better yourself, you'll be far better placed to help others in their lives. Therefore a little bit of selfishness on your part can truly be the best thing for everyone else you know. You don't need a new face, body or lottery win to have a better life. Instead you can do it by simply examining your daily habits, your food, your sleep and even your bowels, and learning the little miracles that can transform every day into a better one. On the way you'll learn how to look better, feel better and stress less. You'll learn to develop a clearer idea of what really matters to you in life and what things you should simply delegate to others so they can help you achieve your own total wellbeing. Just one good idea can point you in the right direction. Fifty-two of them should help point you firmly on your way!

Go well.

Kate Cook

52 Brilliant Ideas – **Get healthy for good**

1
What goes in must come out

Alimentary, my dear Watson. A quick tour of how your digestion works is a useful foundation to health, and a great ice-breaker at parties.

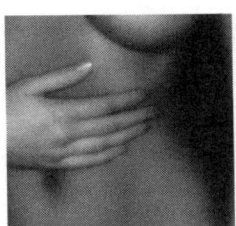

We all know that what goes in at the top comes out in a different form at the bottom. But what happens in between? And why is it so important that all the different components of the digestive system are working properly?

It all starts when you first smell that delicious roast chicken your mum is cooking for dinner. As the aroma wafts up the stairs and into your room and your nostrils, powerful chemical messages are set in motion to get us ready to digest and assimilate food. Chewing food is particularly important in getting enzymes, which break down food, ready for work as the food is passed into the stomach, which acts like a soft-walled concrete mixer. Except, of course, that you're actually churning food in a man-made soup of hydrochloric acid. Far from being a bad thing, this stomach acid is crucial, and poor digestion may be down to not having enough of

> **Here's an idea for you...**
>
> Give your liver a holiday by taking supplements of the herb milk thistle to help it function better. Also drink beetroot juice, which is a liver cleanser. Avoid heavy, fatty foods and take a break from alcohol.

this acid. If you're worried about not having enough, try relaxing at meal times (stress shuts down your digestive system) or get a qualified nutritionist to test your stomach acidity and recommend how to improve your digestive health. There's some controversy about drinking with meals and some experts are actually convinced that liquid waters down your digestive fire, making it less effective. If, like most people, you're worried about having too much stomach acid (reflux, acid burn), check out your lifestyle and diet (drinking too much?) or think about being tested for food intolerances.

GUT FEELING

Once your stomach has finished all that churning, your food is passed to the next bit of the processing machine, your small intestine, which is anything but small. Your food is digested and absorbed here so that you can function. One of the most important organs that helps do all this clever stuff is the pancreas, which neutralises the acid mixture that leaves the stomach and then secretes specific chemicals or enzymes to break down the food into smaller particles.

If you feel that your digestion isn't quite what it should be, why not try food combining? There are massive tomes on this, such as *The Food Combining Bible* by Jan Dries and Inge Dries, but put at its simplest it means eating carbohydrates and proteins at separate meals but never together. You must also eat fruit away from other food. Sir John Mills has been a huge fan of this way of eating for much of his long life. Food combiners say that it does wonders for the digestion, as all the different enzymes aren't competing against each other.

Idea 1 – What goes in must come out

LIVER LITTLE LONGER

It's your liver – a wonder of engineering – that gets the hardest time of all. It helps to emulsify fats and it breaks down hormones, including cholesterol. Your liver manufactures 13,000 chemicals and has 2,000 enzyme systems! You've got to keep it in top nick or you'll start to feel a bit off-colour. I hate to spoil your fun, but drinking is obviously the big baddy in terms of making the liver work harder than it should.

The liver produces fluid called bile, which is stored in the gall bladder. When we eat, the gall bladder and liver release bile into the duct that connects the liver, gall bladder and pancreas to the small intestine. Bile helps emulsify fats, making it easier for them to be digested. An easy supplement to add into your diet is lecithin, which helps your body to emulsify fat. You can even get it from some supermarkets, and your local healthfood store should also oblige.

NEARLY THERE...

The last bit of digestion is when what's left of your grub – by this time mainly water, bacteria and fibre – enters the large intestine. About 12 litres (2.5 gallons) of water pass through the large intestine daily, two-thirds from body fluids alone. The large intestine is where your friendly bacteria live. It's quite a teaming life-centre in there! Friendly bacteria are sensitive little souls, so look after them well by not

Try another idea...

Improving your bowel habits is key to fantastic health. Check out **IDEA 2, *Digestion up close and personal*, and IDEA 13, *Ready for a detox?***

Defining idea...

'The surface area of the digestive mucosae, measuring up and down all the folds, rugae, villi and microvilli, is about the size of tennis court.'
Dr SYDNEY BAKER, giving a simple picture of how your gut is one *big* part of who you are!

getting too stressed and by eating foods that nurture them, like vegetables. They love fibre. You have a responsibility now! Trillions of little lives are depending on you. Apparently, they're so sensitive that they can even be killed off by loud rock music. No wonder poor old Ozzie Osborne is suffering! So, take care of your mini ecopark. In fact, why not increase the friendly bacteria in your gut by getting a good acidophilus supplement? You could try www.biocare.co.uk, which manufactures a range of good products.

We all know what happens next. The large intestine is connected to the anus, where the end product of digestion is excreted. This gives rise to all sorts of jokes and is a particular obsession with the British. In other parts of Europe, examining this end product is seen as a good way to diagnose your internal health. Those German toilet bowls with the handy internal shelf are built like that for a reason. For example, a pale, floating stool could mean you're not digesting fat properly and you could amend your diet to take this into consideration. One way to improve this process is to increase the fibre in your diet by upping the amount of vegetables and fruit that you consume. And don't forget to increase the amount of water you're drinking too. If absolutely nothing is happening in this department or your bowels are very slow, consider supplementing fibre in the diet. Phyllium husk is a good way to do this and is available from health shops.

Idea 1 – **What goes in must come out**

Q **If I 'up' my vegetable intake, I get terrible wind! Any suggestions?**

How did it go?

A Vegetables are a great source of fibre, but the digestive system struggles to digest them. Cooking them lightly or steaming them could help. You could also take a digestive enzyme that contains amyloglucosidase (or glucoamylase), which helps break down a troublesome substance called glucosides, found especially in broccoli, cauliflower and cabbage. Alternatively, you could try charcoal tablets. Not the ones you give dogs, but special ones available from healthfood stores.

Q **How else can I improve my digestion?**

A Chew your food well and avoid eating quickly, eating heavy food late at night and eating indigestible food (lots of red meat). If you're worried about your digestion, a qualified nutritionist can recommend digestive enzymes to suit your needs.

52 Brilliant Ideas – **Get healthy for good**

2

Digestion up close and personal

An inefficient bowel is the genesis of several major degenerative diseases, including cancer. Good health starts with good digestion, so let's take a closer look at yours.

Your bowels need to be working very efficiently in order to remove the body's waste. They reabsorb water to be recycled by the body and without an efficient digestive system the result will be like a washing machine where the wastepipe feeds straight back into the drum.

THE BEET GOES ON

Which brings us to my favourite topic: stools. An important measure of bowel performance is transit time – how long it takes from the time you eat a food until it comes out the other end. The most effective way to measure this is to eat three or four whole beetroots. This is because beetroot can turn the stool bright red and so

Here's an idea for you... Add flax seeds to your morning cereals to help oil the cogs and keep everything regular. Another great general digestive tonic is aloe vera. You can buy it neat, but watch out for the sugar content in some of the aloe vera drinks at healthfood stores.

if you take note of when you eat the beets you can calculate how long your own personal transit time is. Twelve to 24 hours is the optimal transit time. Sweetcorn works well too – you should spot recognisable corn emerging out the other end. If it's less than 12 hours it's possible that you're not absorbing all the nutrients you should be from your food. More than 24 hours indicates that the wastes are sitting inside your bowel for too long and this can greatly increase the risk of colon disease.

If you've done this experiment and found that your transit time is slow, you'll be relieved to hear that all isn't lost:

- One of the major elements in your diet to increase is fibre, and generally you can do this pretty easily by upping the amount of fruit, vegetables and pulses (e.g. lentils) you're eating. Whole grains are also full of fibre, so adding these to your diet will help too. By whole grains I mean unprocessed grains, because processing removes all of the husk and the fibre, which is why brown rice is so much better for you than white. A word of warning though: because of the healthy associations attached to brown bread, some processed loaves are coloured to give them a healthy colour. Look for the key phrase 'wholemeal' to avoid this particular trick. Bread should be heavy and more brick-like – light and fluffy says a lot of air and not much substance.

- Increasing your water intake is vital. Water shortages do for your digestion pretty much what they do for any other living thing.

Idea 2 – Digestion up close and personal

- Foods that react negatively in the gut include sugar, alcohol, high-fat foods and junk foods like chips and pastries, to name but a few of the major culprits. Foods made up of flour are particularly able to slow everything down in there. Remember making glue from flour and water when you were at school? The same principle applies here.

Try another idea...

Check out IDEA 3, *Vital energy*, or IDEA 13, *Ready for a detox?*

FRIEND OR FOE?

Your insides are prime real estate. You have between about 400 and 500 different bacteria living in your bowels. A total of one hundred trillion bacteria live in your entire digestive system comprising a total weight of about four pounds, and the majority of these guys live in your colon. Some kinds of bacteria are goodies, some are baddies and some don't affect our health at all. The trick is not to let the baddies overwhelm our system and cause an imbalance leading to ill health.

The goodies aren't just in there for the ride, they actually have a major effect on our good health. These guys manufacture many vitamins, including from the important B group, and make some minerals more bioavailable. They also help increase our resistance to food poisoning and are a vital part of our immune system. They can even work to prevent tumours and cancers. To get more of these desirable tenants into your system, eat more cultured foods like yoghurt, sauerkraut and cottage cheese. There are also a number of yoghurts now available containing 'live bacteria' (such as bifidus). If yoghurt leaves you cold, you could take a friendly bacteria supplement. Just one tablet can represent the equivalent of fifteen small tubs of yoghurt, which would take a long time to get through using the traditional teaspoon technique!

Defining idea...

'Better out than in.'
ANONYMOUS. Traditional wisdom as relevant today as it ever was

9

How did it go?

Q **Food just seems to sit in my tummy after I've eaten. It doesn't feel like it's being digested. Is there anything I can do?**

A You could look into the Hay Diet, commonly referred to as food combining. It isn't great for blood sugar problems, but people with digestive issues swear by it. The main principle is don't mix carbohydrates and proteins at the same meal. The diet comes under a lot of stick from conventional circles disputing the scientific evidence for its success, but it has had many high-profile devotees, including Sir John Mills, who would say that the evidence speaks for itself. For more details read The Food Combining Bible by Jan and Inge Dries.

Q **I'm eating all the right stuff so why is nothing moving down there?**

A Are you suffering from stress? Stress levels need to be controlled because if your body thinks you're in mortal danger, your fight or flight mechanisms will shut down digestion. You might also try supplementing with a digestive enzyme, under the advice of a nutritional therapist.

3
Vital energy

We need an endless supply of energy to do everything we need and want to do in our lives, yet we're often overwhelmed by a desire to have a swift forty winks.

Have you ever felt like curling up under your desk and spending the afternoon snoozing? Or been in serious need of matchsticks to prop your eyelids open? And do you ever wonder why this always seems to happen in the middle of a vital meeting, despite three cups of coffee?

THE ENERGY EQUATION

We need sugar (glucose) to fire our system. It's the fuel that gives us our energy. However, too much is deemed by our body to be dangerous (think of diabetics).

We obtain this fuel largely from our food. A hormone called insulin specifically lowers these blood sugar levels and adjusts them according to our minute-by-minute needs. We don't have very much sugar circulating at any one time because

Here's an idea for you...

Get a good breakfast in! A recent study revealed that people who didn't eat breakfast were likely to be overweight and less intelligent. So, if you didn't have a good reason before, you have now. A good breakfast will sustain you through to lunch, but remember that sugary cereals will pick you up and then drop you like a stone.

as soon as we do, in comes insulin to normalise the level. When blood sugar levels are low, we rely on stored glucose (glycogen) found in the muscles and the liver, which helps maintain this delicate equilibrium. Once stored glucose is used, more food will be required to sustain glucose production.

Not all food was created equal. Some foods 'burn' (meaning they're converted into sugar) quickly while other foods 'burn' slowly. These foods are called low and high glycaemic index foods (GI foods). The GI index is a way of measuring foods that are converted to glucose at different rates. But don't get hung up on the GI index, as confusingly you'll see it published in different places with different values. As a very simple rule of thumb, white things (e.g. potatoes, pasta, bread, parsnips, white rice) are like rocket fuel while dense, thick, fibrous, brown or green things (e.g. lentils, chickpeas, broccoli, brown rice) are going to burn more slowly and are our great energy sustainers. For example, whereas glucose (sugar) scores 100 on the GI scale, a lentil comes in at a cool 42. The important thing to remember is that it isn't necessarily foods that we traditionally think of as sweet that cause the problems. A 'sweet' potato, for instance, actually scores quite low, as it is wonderfully fibrous.

You can raise your blood sugar by another mechanism. Stick your head in the mouth of a man-eating shark, then quickly take it out again and swim like hell for the shore. This would certainly pick your blood sugar up rapidly, as powerful stress

Idea 3 – **Vital energy**

hormones would raise blood sugar to give you enough energy for your clever exit strategy. We do this all the time, but usually our boss, gas bill or deadline is the cause of our stress and not man-eating sharks. Of course there is an easier way of picking up blood sugar levels – have a fag or a cup of coffee. These are both stimulants, which stimulate the adrenal glands (where those stress hormones come from) to release sugar from storage. But what goes up, must come down, hence staying awake in the meeting becomes a challenge.

So, what's the problem with the blood sugar whizzing up and down all the time? First, the pancreas, where all that insulin is produced is going to get worn out. Second, you're going to get dips of energy as the blood sugar levels plummet when insulin tries to lower them. Third, insulin is also a fat storage hormone, so if it overreacts and there's continuously too much insulin in the system, eventually you'll put on weight. Commonly this appears as those cute love handles or that attractive tyre round the middle. And where do you see this phenomenon most commonly? On stressed out executives who are eating the wrong things, having too many cups of coffee and getting stressed out.

> **For ideas on what to eat see IDEA 18, *What does a day look like?***

Try another idea...

> '*Mary: I want a guy who can play 36 holes of golf, and still have enough energy to take Warren and me to a baseball game, and eat sausages, and beer, not lite beer, but beer. That's my ad, print it up.*
> *Brenda: "Fatty who likes golf, beer, and baseball." Gee, Mary, where are you gonna find a gem like that?*'
> THERE'S SOMETHING ABOUT MARY, a lesson in why you should be careful how you define 'energy'

Defining idea...

13

How did it go?

Q **I'm starving by 11.00 a.m. How do I avoid stuffing my face with chocolate?**

A Make sure you really are getting a good breakfast. By that I mean one with a low GI score. Good foods for breakfast include eggs with rye toast, sardines on toast, yoghurt with ground nuts and seeds, and porridge oats with fruit, nuts and seeds.

Q **What if I don't have the time for cooking?**

A Making breakfast is really quick once you get organised and get the right foods in. Unless you're very keen, you might not want to bring your lunch into work in a Tupperware container. You might have to find lunch on the hoof. Although a baked potato has a high GI score, a little protein brings it down so add some cottage cheese or tuna. Dinner is easy to organise – steam some vegetables and grill some fish or chicken. Start looking at recipe books for inspiration – you don't actually have to follow them to the letter. Once you're used to cooking, it really is quicker than opening a packet.

Q **What if I don't have the time to go shopping?**

A Have you tried shopping on line? Once it's set up it's wonderfully easy. Ones that promise hour delivery slots are best, otherwise you have to hang around for them to deliver, which is a pain. The key phrase is, 'Be prepared.'

Idea 3 – **Vital energy**

52 Brilliant Ideas – **Get healthy for good**

4
Stressed out

You rarely realise how stressed you are till the day you chew the head off a shop assistant for taking too long at the till. However, when you do lose your cool like this, it's time to admit you've got a problem.

Up until the point you really lost it, you probably thought it was the shop assistant with the problem. After all, they're the one who can't count the change without moving their lips, right?

Be careful how you voice this problem. Well-meaning friends and family members will suddenly get ultraconcerned. They tell you to relax, take it easy, breathe deeply, go out for long walks. You smile through gritted teeth. Don't these people know how busy you are? You have no time for all this namby-pamby relaxation nonsense. You have to get on.

Stress is dealt with in various chapters in this book, but right here, right now, is there anything you can do to elevate your mood? At least so you don't snap at friends when they give you all that advice on destressing.

Here's an idea for you... **Eat several snacks during the day rather than three great big meals. This will prevent too many massive peaks and dips in your blood sugar level so you'll be able to step off that blood sugar rollercoaster. Choosing the right kind of food to snack on is key. Protein is low on the GI Index and doesn't just mean great slabs of meat. Snack on nuts and seeds – almonds and sunflower or pumpkin seeds are ideal. Or try oatcakes with goat's cheese, hummus or cottage cheese. And if this doesn't appeal, fruit with yoghurt is always an option.**

WHAT CAN I DO?

Well, one thing you can do immediately is balance your blood sugar levels. Don't panic! Put thoughts of diabetes and daily injections out of your mind. You can do this through what you eat and once you've got the hang of it, it's like falling off a log. We all have to balance our blood sugar levels to a greater or lesser degree, depending on how our body handles the sugar (glucose) in the blood. Very simplistically, sweet things or fast energy-releasing foods will send your blood sugar levels soaring high like a rocket and then crashing rapidly down again once the hormone insulin rushes in to lower the sugar in the blood. The trick is to choose foods that sustain you. Dense, fibrous foods such as lentils do this rather than sweet or starchy foods like gluey white loaves of bread or potatoes. Eat slow energy-releasing carbohydrates, or protein with slow energy-releasing carbohydrates, which will raise blood sugar levels slowly.

So, what effect does wildly fluctuating blood sugar levels have on mood? Well, in case your partner hasn't told you already, this can make you irritable, grouchy and fatigued. Not great things to aspire to if you want to handle your stress better.

Idea 4 – **Stressed out**

ALLERGY, ALLERGY EVERYWHERE

Food intolerances, referred to by some as food allergies, seem to be all the rage these days. Generally speaking, an example of a food allergy is if you fall down gasping when you eat nuts. A food intolerance can have loads of different effects on the health, but you may feel anything from a general unwell feeling to aching joints. It may also affect your mood. If you suspect you might have a problem then visit a nutritionist.

FAT HEAD

Omega-3 and omega-6 fats are called essential fats because they are. Essential that is. Your body's hormones and your brain run on them so if you make sure you're getting enough. Sources of omega-3 fats include flax and hemp seeds, whereas omega-6 fats come from oily fish like sardines, mackerel or salmon. The brain is more than 60% fat.

FOOD AND MOOD

An easy way to improve how you deal with stress is to reduce the amount of tea and coffee you drink. These contain stimulants that only make you more hyped up and tense. Try cutting down on those lattes and see how you feel.

Try another idea...

There's loads to look at regarding mood and stress, but for starters why not check out IDEA 45, *You have one day to live!*, and IDEA 48, *Breathe in, breathe out*! For more on blood sugar levels, see IDEA 3, *Vital energy*.

Defining idea...

'You are what you eat.'
ANONYMOUS

19

If you thought that tryptophan was a village in Wales, I'm afraid you're wrong. Tryptophan is an amino acid (protein building block) that can help raise levels of the mood-boosting neurotransmitter serotonin. Foods high in tryptophan include figs, milk, tuna, chicken, seaweed, sunflower seeds and yoghurt, but you need to make sure you have plenty of B vitamins in place for your body to process it (especially B3, B6, folic acid and biotin). You also need vitamin C and zinc. Eating some slow energy-releasing carbohydrates with a tryptophan-rich food also helps your body process the tryptophan and turn it into serotonin.

How did it go?

Q **I thought that a good stiff gin and tonic would improve my mood, but I began to feel sleepy instead. What's going on?**

A Alcohol raises blood sugar levels rapidly. The sleepiness that follows is a blood sugar slump. Alcohol may seem relaxing, but it can sometimes make us just a little too relaxed.

Q **I suppose reaching for a chocolate bar when I'm stressed isn't a good idea either?**

A I'm afraid not. Apart from being high in fat, chocolate also sends your blood sugar levels soaring. This may seem like a quick fix, but will only leave you crashing down and wanting more later.

5
What's in what?

Which foods should you target for good health? Here's a quick guide to what's in your food.

The key to a great diet is variety. This will ensure that you get a broad spectrum of nutrients — vitamins and minerals for everyday health.

A NUTRITIONAL RAINBOW

The rule of thumb is to eat as many different coloured foods as possible throughout the day. Coloured food is full of nutrients – look for reds, greens, yellows, oranges and all the colours in between. These will give you antioxidant vitamins that can protect you from disease. A broad spectrum of vitamins and minerals is really important.

I'm not going to go through every vitamin and mineral here, but I'd like to highlight the B group of vitamins, which are very important to our nervous system. They're found in a wide array of foods, but particularly in grains. I'd also like to

Here's an idea for you... Why not try a rotation diet? It doesn't have to be overly complicated. Choose a different grain for each of the five working days. So, Monday might be your wheat day, Tuesday your oat day, Wednesday your rice day, Thursday your millet day and Friday your rye day. Try to consume just the allotted grains on each of these days. In this way you'll be automatically varying your diet.

highlight vitamin C, which is found in berries, citrus fruits, tomatoes and potatoes. Of the minerals, a key one to top up on is calcium, which is found in almonds, sesame seeds and vegetables (that's where cows get their calcium from to provide calcium-rich milk). Among other things, we need calcium for bone and teeth formation, as well as nerve and muscle function. Zinc is another top mineral as it's essential to most bodily functions, including fertility and brain function. Zinc is found in shellfish, lentils, pumpkin seeds and eggs. Before we leave this lightning tour of vitamins and minerals I'd like to mention selenium, another mineral worthy of top billing.

Selenium is another antioxidant and it may help prevent cancer. It's naturally found in wheat germ, tomatoes, onions, broccoli, garlic, eggs, liver and seafood. If you want to know more about vitamins and minerals and where to find them, a great book worth investing in is *The Optimum Nutrition Bible* by Patrick Holford. It's a good, easy and informative read.

So, why do we need vitamins? Well, they're essential to life. They contribute to good health by assisting the biochemical mechanisms in the body and help metabolism. They're considered micronutrients, as the body needs them in tiny amounts to make everything run smoothly. Vitamins work with enzymes to make functions work in the body. There are two main categories: water-soluble vitamins, which

Idea 5 – What's in what?

must be taken into the body daily, and oil-based vitamins, which can be stored (these include vitamins, A, C, E and K). Minerals come in different forms. The major minerals, such as calcium, magnesium and potassium, form part of the structure of bones and organs. These are needed either in high milligrams or even gram quantities on a daily basis. Then there are the trace elements, which are important for biochemical reactions in the body. Become deficient in any of these and eventually some part of your body will begin to grind to a halt.

Variation in the diet is the key to expanding the possibility of a wide choice of vitamins and minerals. Due to modern methods of transporting and storing food, even the freshest food can be nutrient deficient. Mineral levels in food are decreasing at an alarming rate because their soils are becoming depleted. You may wish to supplement your diet with a good multivitamin and mineral supplement. A qualified nutritionist will help you make a good choice.

Try another idea...

Check out IDEA 7, *Superfoods*, and IDEA 20, *Nutrition: the basics*.

Defining idea...

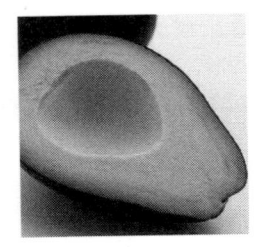

'Nurture your mind with great thoughts.'
BENJAMIN DISRAELI

How did it go?

Q **What if I don't like vegetables very much? I was put off at school where they gave us cabbage that had been boiled to death.**

A *I find that cooking vegetables in interesting new ways really helps. I gently steam-fry lots of vegetables together with masses of herbs, ginger and lemon grass. Sometimes I use Indian or Thai recipes to make vegetables into a veritable feast of gorgeous colours, tastes and smells. Vegetables need never be boring!*

Q **I think I eat a balanced diet, whatever that means. Will I be getting all the vitamins and minerals I need for good health?**

A *You say, 'whatever that means' and you've got it in one! No one will define this mythical balanced diet, so how do you know if you personally are getting one? Variety is the spice of life. Eat all sorts of grains and fruit, different coloured vegetables, different kinds of oily fish and, if you eat meat, good organic meat occasionally. Because of modern farming methods that deplete the soil of nutrients, in the West we're not malnourished in terms of calories but we are malnourished in terms of nutrients. There might be some merit in choosing a good multivitamin, such as Solgar's VM2000. However, remember that most supplements are produced chemically. I'm therefore a great fan of superfoods, and Perfect Food capsules or powder by Garden of Life (www.gardenoflife.com) are a good choice.*

6

Get organic

With more and more headlines screaming at us every day about unsafe food, is it any wonder that we're turning to organic food in our droves? But is it worth it?

From pesticide residue in pears to mercury poisoning from tuna, it's no wonder we're unsure about what's safe. But aside from this, we're turning to organic because of the taste. Remember how tomatoes should taste? Quite simply, like organic ones.

PRODUCTION MEANS PRIZES

Farmers have been under a huge amount of pressure to increase productivity, but at a cost. Many nonorganic fruit and vegetables contain a wide range of weedkillers, pesticides and fertilizers to increase food production. Fruit and vegetables also have to look perfect for supermarkets to accept them. Gnarled or pitted products are simply not accepted. But what effects do these chemicals have on human health?

Here's an idea for you...

If you can't afford to go the whole organic hog, then prioritise. The government advises that carrots, apples and pears should be peeled as they absorb insecticides through the skin, which could make them unsafe. Buying organic could be a better option. Conventionally farmed salmon are treated with pesticides to prevent mite infestations and there are fears that the chemicals become concentrated in the fish. And choose organic milk and beef, as 'normal' cows are in some countries treated with hormones and other growth promoters.

It seems that we know that pesticide residues can cause anxiety, hyperactivity, digestive problems and muscle weakness. Children are particularly vulnerable, as their immune systems aren't fully up and running and their comparatively small body mass means that chemicals are more concentrated.

And it's not just fruit and vegetables that we have to worry about. The biggest risks and the biggest worries come in the form of meat products: crazy cows, potty pigs – it's no joke. The many years of intensive farming in crowded conditions has reaped a whole host of health concerns. It's just not possible to crowd animals into such tight spaces without using industrial strength chemical agents to get rid of the threat of spreading disease.

FEEDING ON DEMAND

We're so used to having exotic fruit and vegetables out of season and on demand that at first it's difficult to accept that we can only get organic fruit and vegetables that are in season. Of course, a lot of organic food is produced abroad and flown to our supermarkets and this makes it more available, but vitamins and mineral content is lost if food has been on a long journey. It's therefore much better to buy locally produced products if you can. Many supermarkets are cottoning on to the fact that organic means *big* business. But remember that just because it says its organic on the packet, it doesn't mean that it's better for you, especially if it has been processed. Once organic products have been turned into a crisp, cake or biscuit, for example, you'll have more or less the same concerns attached to the conventional versions of these foods: high sugar and fat. So don't be had!

Worth a look at are IDEA 5, What's in what, and IDEA 7, Superfoods.

Try another idea...

EXPECT THE INSPECTION

The term 'organic' is defined in law and can only be used by farmers who have an organic licence. These farmers have to follow guidelines on how to produce food to organic standards and they're inspected regularly to make sure that these standards are being met. Visit www.soilassociation.org to find out the ins and outs of organic certification in the UK.

Do I buy organic foods? Yes, and I think it's worth it. I always make sure that any meat, eggs or fish is organic and I get organic fruit and vegetables when they're available. I have a box delivered to my door. You'll probably find details of an organic home delivery company at your local healthfood shop. I'm now very aware of what fruit and vegetables are in season. And instead of looking in a recipe book and going out to buy what I need, I simply look in the box and create my menus around what I'm given.

'Organic farming delivers the highest quality, best-tasting food, produced without artificial chemicals or genetic modification and with respect for animal welfare and the environment, while helping to maintain the landscape and rural communities.'
PRINCE CHARLES, a big fan of organic food

Defining idea...

27

52 Brilliant Ideas – **Get healthy for good**

How did it go?

Q **I'm on a tight budget and organic food is too expensive. What can I do about all those pesticides?**

A *If you can't afford to buy organic, add a generous splash of vinegar to the water when you're giving your vegetables a scrub. There are also products that claim to remove pesticides from your fruit and vegetables – visit www.vegiwash.com to find out more.*

Q **Any other ways to save money?**

A *There are farmers' markets springing up everywhere. These are full of locally grown produce. All products sold are grown, reared, caught, pickled, baked, smoked or processed by the stallholder. Go at the end of the day, when the stallholders often sell produce more cheaply.*

7

Superfoods

What exactly are superfoods? Comic-book heroes with a mission to save the world?

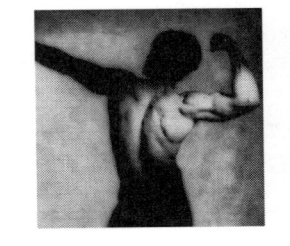

In their own small way superfoods are indeed our own personal superheroes, as they're foods that have beneficial effects on our health.

Often the best way to get the best from these superfoods is to juice them so that their goodness is easy to absorb. Let's run through a few of the top superfoods that you could incorporate into your juicing repertoire. Well, 'a' is for apple and unsurprisingly apples are a number one superfood. In fact, the well-known herbalist Maurice Messegue once said, 'If you could plant only one tree in your garden, it should be an apple tree.' So, now you know. Apples contain plenty of vitamin C, and the pectin in apples helps keep cholesterol levels stable. Pectin also protects us from pollution. On top of all this, the malic and tartaric acid in apples help neutralise the acid by-products of indigestion and help your body cope with dietary excesses.

Here's an idea for you...

Consider taking superfoods in powder form – you can get a day's worth of vegetable requirements in one drink. The only downside is that they have an 'interesting' earthy flavour, but don't let that put you off. It could be my imagination, but I swear I feel a definite zing when I drink mine every morning! Check out www.gardenoflifeusa.com or www.kiki-health.com.

Beetroot was used in Romany medicine as a blood-builder for patients who looked pale and run down. Don't overdo it though, as beetroot is such a powerful detoxicant that too much could be a strain on your system. Broccoli is another big superhero. It has been demonstrated in a number of studies to have a protective effect against cancer. And yet another superfood is the humble carrot. Carrots are so rich in betacarotene that a single carrot will supply a whole day's worth of vitamin A requirements. Carrots are also a number one cancer protector.

A great ingredient to add into a juice is a little bit of ginger. Ginger is anti-inflammatory, helps colds and flu and chest congestion, and has been used for centuries as a remedy against sickness and nausea. Another great additive to a juice is parsley, which is full of vitamins A and C and bursting with manganese, iron, copper, calcium, phosphorous, sodium, potassium and magnesium. It acts as a blood purifier.

Although I've picked out just a few here, most fruit and vegetables are of course superfoods. Each and every one has some benefit to our health. Sometimes there are surprises – a kiwi, for example, contains twice as much vitamin C as an orange. And pineapples have both an antibiotic and anti-inflammatory effect. Mother Nature is simply amazing!

Idea 7 - **Superfoods**

SQUEEZE ME!

So how can you obtain the amazing health benefits from superfoods? Why not try your hand at juicing? Some people think this is a better way than vitamin pills to get your nutrition, as juice is easy to assimilate into the body and it's in the natural form the body can recognise. If you're serious about juicing, invest in a really good juicer like a Champion Juicer (www.championjuicer.com). Further juicers can be found at www.wholisticresearch.com.

What health bonuses do you get by juicing? Well, fruit and vegetable juices are absolutely packed with enzymes, which are vital for digestion, brain stimulation and cellular energy. They're also packed with phytochemicals, which are linked with disease-busting properties. Juice is also a concentrated supply of nutrients, which juice you up with energy! And as if this wasn't enough, juices help to balance acid and alkaline in the body – over-acidity is the root cause of many health problems. Stress also produces a lot of acid compounds in the body and juices help to neutralise these.

Juicing is the number one weapon in your detox armoury. Detoxing isn't a solution to every health challenge, but it can have a powerful effect on cleansing the body and establishing a foundation for health.

Try another idea...
If you're interested in food – and who isn't – read IDEA 6, *Get organic*, and IDEA 5, *What's in what?* Read IDEA 13, *Ready for a detox?*, and get really into juicing.

Defining idea...
'One that would have the fruit must climb the tree.'
THOMAS FULLER, by the time you've bought the fruit, cut it up, juiced it, drunk it and cleaned the juicer, you've certainly 'climbed the tree'

52 Brilliant Ideas – **Get healthy for good**

How did it go?

Q **I can't be bothered to make juices. Isn't there an easier way?**

A   Yes! Cleaning the juicer can really be a pain, but there are hundreds of juice bars springing up so get your juices to order. Alternatively, buy them already made up – organic juices are best!

Q **If I'm new to juicing, what type of vegetable should I start with?**

A   Start with carrots, which go with any other vegetable and mix nicely with apple juice too. Choose fruit and vegetables that are in season because they're the sweetest and ripest and therefore contain the most vitamins, minerals and enzymes.

8
Eat fat

Shops are full of low-fat everything, from cookies and cakes to yoghurt and tofu. In fact, the body desperately needs fats, but only the right kind will do.

Fat has practically become a four-letter word, certainly a feminist issue and definitely public enemy number one. But the new thinking is that fat is your friend — so embrace it. There's one small catch — you must make sure that it is the right kind of fat.

We have a complex about fat. So ingrained is the message of how fat clogs up our arteries, increases our apple-shaped girths, sends our risk of heart disease soaring and is linked to the hooded claw that is cholesterol. The expression 'a moment on the lips a lifetime on the hips' was probably specifically invented for this fat phobia.

The impression given by health writers in the 80s and 90s was that fat was definitely public enemy number one. There were well-meaning diet gurus writing books telling us to avoid it at all costs. However, all fat was not created equal and as

Here's an idea for you...

You probably get enough omega-6 as the Western diet tends to be omega-6 heavy, but you could get extra from nuts and seeds – grind some (sesame, pumpkin and sunflower) in a coffee grinder and add them to your morning cereal. To get enough omega-3, up your oily fish quota (salmon, herring, mackerel or sardines). If you're vegetarian you could add a flax seed oil supplement to your diet. There are hundreds of good supplement companies, but you could try the widely available brand Solgar (www.solgar.com).

we are finding out to our cost, avoiding all kinds of fat is detrimental to our health.

Oil in its unprocessed form is highly perishable and before man moved en masse into the towns, oil used to be sold fresh door to door. Although this is hard to believe nowadays due to the highly processed yellow cooking oils available in supermarkets, if oil wasn't kept cool it would go off and be rancid in a matter of days. The advertising boys have managed to persuade us that we should go for the polyunsaturated or cholesterol-free oils, but these oils have often been refined very highly using high heat and bleaches that strip them of any nutritional value and may in fact make them unstable and potentially toxic.

The chemical building blocks that oils are made up of are called fatty acids, and the fatty acids that are essential to human health and cannot be manufactured by the body are called essential fatty acids or EFAs. As their name would suggest, these oils really are essential to human health and without them we'd be on the fast track to degenerative disease.

Idea 8 – **Eat fat**

EFAs have a more than magical effect on our health and wellbeing. Our skin is waterproofed with oil, and our hormones and brains work with it. In fact, the brain is more than 60% fat, which makes the insult 'fat head' actually quite a compliment. The list of essential fats' great benefits to humankind is really quite impressive. They improve skin and hair condition, aid in the prevention of arthritis and lower cholesterol levels, and that's just for starters. They're also helpful in terms of heart disease and eczema, they reduce inflammation in the body and help in the transmission of nerve impulses in the brain. Your body is made up of tiny individual cells, each one crying out for EFAs to make the machine of your body operate. On top of all this, EFAs may help to reduce the likelihood of getting a harmful blood clot.

The two basic groups of EFAs are omega-3 and omega-6 groups. Omega-6 is found mostly in raw nuts, seeds, legumes and in unsaturated oils such as evening primrose oil or sesame oil. Omega-3 is found mainly in fresh deep-water fish, some vegetable oils, flaxseed oil and walnut oil. You mum was right, fish does make you brainy!

Having said all this, the one thing you don't do is cook with essential fats as they're highly unstable. The heat destroys the fatty acids and worse it results in dangerous chemical agents called free radicals, which sounds like something out of *Star Wars*. Better to cook with olive oil, which isn't an essential fat, but a monounsaturated fat that takes higher temperatures to damage it.

Try another idea...
To see how EFAs can make you beautiful too, see IDEA 10, Skin from within.

Defining idea...
'May understanding of health be the starship of the next generation. May the worship of disease die with us.'
UDO ERASMUS, oil guru and clearly a fellow *Star Wars* fan

THE FAT GURU

The guru of fats is someone by the name of Udo Erasmus who knows all there is to know about oils and what they do for you. In his book *Fats that Heal, Fats that kill*, fats are examined in some considerable detail. He says that EFAs should be consumed in a ratio of about 3:1 to 5:1 for omega-6 and omega-3 respectively. Reality is that nowadays we consume a ratio of 10:1 to 20:1. We're cruising for a bruising in health terms as our bodies struggle to use the wrong ratio of fuel to power our system.

How did it go?

Q **Someone told me that because I pee a lot and get really thirsty I have an EFA deficiency. Is that true?**

A It could be, as without a good lot of EFAs your body can't regulate water balance efficiently. The body is about 66% water so we need to keep it in our bodies, rather than it evaporating. However, thirst and peeing a lot can be a sign of blood sugar imbalance too or even diabetes, so if you're worried consult your doctor.

Q **I'm worried I don't get enough omega-3 because I hate fish. Is there another good source?**

A Yes, seeds and seed oils. Try Udo's Oil (by the guru himself), which is blended to give a full omega-3/6 balance and to be acceptable for vegetarians.

9
What's bothering you?

What do you think are the top three complaints dealt with in my clinic on a day-to-day basis?

At number one is irritable bowel syndrome (IBS). Second on the list is premenstrual syndrome (PMS) and this is followed closely by people feeling low, depressed and anxious.

The general rule is that if you know something isn't quite right, check it out with a doctor. Doctors are fabulous diagnosticians and it's much better to know that you were making a fuss about nothing, than leaving something too late. Then you can choose what to do about that diagnosis.

Read all you can about your condition – get on the internet and see what other people are doing about it. Ring up your friends and see if they know what to do about it. If you've gone to the doctor and they've diagnosed a particular condition, challenge them. Ask them why they have the opinion they have and what you can do about it. Get all the options. It's your health and your responsibility – don't hand that responsibility to anyone else. It's in your hands and you'll nearly always be in a

Here's an idea for you...

Do just one thing today to improve your health. Add a piece of fruit to your diet, go for a walk or get to a yoga class. Keep up that change for one month, which should be enough to make it a permanent habit. A great book on this is Andrew Weil's *Eight Weeks to Optimum Health*, plus he has a fabulous website at www.myoptimumhealthplan.com.

position to improve your circumstances, from improving your diet to improving your lifestyle. Make the right choices and you'll generally see your health improve.

QUICK FIX

The thing about natural health is that it can take a while for your health to improve. Due to the very nature of our quick-fix society, we're usually in a real rush to solve the problem and move on, but we have to train ourselves to be more Zen about our health – 'infinite' patience is the slogan here. Ever watched a Zen monk raking his gravel garden? Watching paint dry would make better live TV, but to the monk the understanding of effort and reward make the whole process transfixing. We're so used to the process of going to the doctor, getting the pill and being cured that we find it difficult to give natural medicine the time it needs to work. Taking a pill doesn't cure us, it's simply

Defining idea...

'Those in a hurry do not arrive.'
Zen saying, on the virtues of patience

Idea 9 – What's bothering you?

masking the symptoms. Often taking the pill can lead to a cascade of other problems too. Of course, there is a time and a place for taking pills. Your body will heal itself and get better with a little help from a doctor, a nutritionist, a homeopath, a acupuncturist or whoever, but the most important person in your health team is you.

To get your health on the right track look at IDEA 3, *Vital energy*.

Try another idea...

FEELING LOW

It is possible to improve your mood with your diet. Fresh fruit and vegetables are key factors here. Avoiding stimulants like tea, coffee and cigarettes will stop any blood sugar swings. And look at taking a good multivitamin and a B complex to nurture your nervous system.

How did it go?

Q **I get terrible constipation and diarrhoea, and my doctor has diagnosed IBS. What does this mean?**

A It means that something is irritating your gut. You have to find out what. The best thing to do is to go to a qualified nutritionist who should be able to determine the cause. Often food intolerance is a factor – one or more foods might be bothering your gut. Sometimes wheat and dairy products are the culprits, but it's best to find out precisely what's going on before jumping to any conclusions. Doing a stool test can determine whether parasites or bacterial infections are to blame. Also, take a close look at your stress levels, as stress is a major cause of IBS partly because there are so many nerve endings in the gut.

Q **I'm really grouchy and bad-tempered around my period. My doctor says it's PMS. Is there something I can do to help myself?**

A Improving your diet will really help, so add lots of fresh fruit and vegetables. Make sure you're consuming plenty of essential fatty acids (EFAs), which are found in oily fish and nuts and seeds. Grind up some nuts and seeds and put them on your cereal (high in zinc, magnesium and EFAs). You should consider taking a B complex vitamin supplement, with plenty of B6, and make sure you're taking a multivitamin with zinc in it, which helps convert B6 into its active form. Evening primrose oil, starflower oil or blackcurrant seed oil are all a good source of the EFAs you need.

10
Skin from within

With great nutrition and a little care, you can achieve great-looking skin in no time at all.

If you're anything like the rest of the population, how you look will be very important to you. We worry endlessly about the image we present to the world and a very important part of this is how our skin looks.

TUTTI FRUTTI

You probably don't need me to tell you that fruit and vegetables are the main ingredients to a healthy, youthful skin. The reason for this is that they contain lots of vitamins and minerals that perform an antioxidant function. Antioxidants mop up reactions caused by free radicals, which are unstable molecules created by such things as stress, pollution and certain foods. Free radicals sound like a new political party that we should all be voting for, but instead they're electrochemically unbalanced chemicals which ultimately can be the cause of degenerative diseases

> **Here's an idea for you...**
>
> Try to eat at least five portions of fruit and vegetables daily. And the more colours the better – try red peppers, yellow peppers, green peppers, red cabbage, sweet potatoes, etc. This way you can get enough antioxidants to help counter the effects of pollution. Be sure to buy organic though, as otherwise you could add to your toxic load!

such as cancer and heart disease, not to mention premature ageing (which is where your skin comes in). The main antioxidant vitamins are vitamins A, C and E together with the minerals selenium, manganese and zinc. Some B vitamins also have antioxidant properties together with some amino acids (building blocks for protein). Most of these important minerals can be found in a wholefood, fresh food diet.

Berries and fruits and vegetables with red, purple and blue colouring are particularly good because they're stuffed with antioxidants and contain a group of flavonoids called anthocyanidins, thought to be much more powerful than vitamin E. Antioxidants sometimes work together. For example, vitamins C and E work together – vitamin C allows vitamin E to be recycled in the body so that it can carry on working longer.

WATER YOUR FACE DAILY

Drinking pure, fresh water flushes toxins through your system and hydrates cells carrying essential nutrients to every part of your body. I probably didn't need to tell you that either. Aim to drink about 2 litres (3.5 pints) daily. Don't overdo it though or you could end up flushing minerals out of your system, especially if you're gulping rather than sipping.

Idea 10 – **Skin from within**

FAT FACE!

The other essential ingredient to healthy skin is fat. Not any old fat, but essential fatty acids (EFAs). One group of EFAs is especially important: omega-3. EFAs work as a kind of waterproofer because they stop fluids escaping from your body's cells. In this way, your skin is kept plumped up and moisturised. Do an experiment – take a good quality fish oil supplement for three months (or flax seed if you're vegetarian) and note the quality of skin on the back of your hands. You'll notice that they're better moisturised!

You should also decrease the amount of saturated and processed fats in your diet, as these compete with the good fats and make their job more difficult. In general, the fresher the food and the more unprocessed it is, the wider the vitamin and mineral range and the more good it will do your skin!

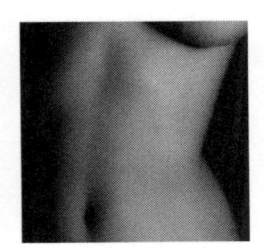

Related ideas to check out are IDEA 8, *Eat fat***, IDEA 36,** *Let's face facts***, and IDEA 6,** *Get organic***.**

Try another idea...

'**All the beauty in the world, 'tis but skin deep.'**
RALPH VENNING

Defining idea...

43

How did it go?

Q **If fruit is so important for my skin, when can I fit in eating more fruit during the day?**

A A great time to load up the fruit content is with your morning breakfast. I load up fruit on my morning oats – I tend to buy packs of blueberries, strawberries and raspberries. Make sure you wash soft fruit well as it's particularly bad for pesticide residues. You can buy frozen berries in most supermarkets and these are great for getting your flavonoids. You can, of course, snack on fruit at any time of the day – my favourite snack is an apple with a few nuts and seeds.

Q **If I'm going to eat all these vegetables, I'm going to be doing a lot of chopping and preparing. Any tips to make this easier?**

A I find that if I buy all my food supplies on Saturday and use Sunday for preparation, it's a lot easier for me to be ready for my week. Chop up all your main salad ingredients, such as red peppers, spring onion, grated carrot, salad leaves, and put them in ziplock bags, making sure that all the air is out (a little squeeze of lemon juice helps keep them fresh). Although not perfect from a purist's point of view because it's always best to chop vegetables as near to when you're going to eat them as possible, in my view it's better to do something rather than nothing and this is a great way to cut down on preparation time.

Idea 10 – **Skin from within**

45

52 Brilliant Ideas – **Get healthy for good**

11
Water babies

Seventy per cent of the planet is covered in water, and when we're born 70% of us is water too. It's cool to be wet, so why aren't you drinking enough of the stuff?

There are life forms that can live without oxygen, but none last long without water. So why do we pay so little attention to it?

Do you know what constantly amazes me? People who go to a posh restaurant, spend a fortune on the meal and then think they're being clever by asking for a glass of tap water. Granted, some places seem to charge more for water than for wine, but is this a smart way of saving money? Most tap water tastes disgusting. I realise that this is my personal opinion, so do your own survey. The most unpalatable glass I ever had was in England's rural Oxfordshire. It was like drinking part of a swimming pool. Even London water tastes better despite, so legend has it, having passed through eight other bodies first. However, is changing to bottled water the solution?

Here's an idea for you...

If you find 2-litre bottles of water too intimidating, try the small ½-litre bottles instead. If you're not used to drinking masses of water, increase your intake slowly by just one ½-litre bottle a day at first. If it feels like trying to rehydrate hard-baked earth after a drought, add some lecithin into your diet as this will help make your cells more permeable to water.

BOTTLED BLISS?

Bottled water isn't always the purest water. In fact, it might actually contain more bacteria than the tap version. Most tap water, however, will contain a cocktail of contaminates, most commonly lead, aluminium and pesticides. Also, the labelling on bottled water makes it far from clear in terms of what you're getting.

Generally, water can be called natural mineral water, spring water or table water. Mineral water is generally from a pure, underground source, where the rocks and earth have naturally filtered it. Spring water also comes from a filtered underground source, but does not have to be bottled on the spot. Table water is definitely the dodgiest dude of all as it's the least defined and could be a mix of water including tap water so unless you really like the design of the bottle you could just be wasting your money. Watch out for artificially carbonated table and spring water as this can rob the vital minerals in the body by binding to them. Also, look at the proportion of minerals – remember that salt (sodium) will dehydrate the body slightly.

Idea 11 – Water babies

Every now and then, there'll be a TV programme featuring blokes turning into women or male fish turning into female fish. Scare stories aside, the point is that we're being continuously exposed to xeno-oestrogens (foreign oestrogens) in our environment and these can have a feminising effect on our bodies. One source of these foreign oestrogens is through plastics – the worst thing you can do is leave your water heating up in the sun in a plastic bottle. So, blokes shouldn't simply blame their boobs on beer (although alcohol also has feminising effects, but that's another story!).

> **As we all know, the key to beautiful skin is to drink plenty of water. Check out IDEA 10, Skin from within.**
>
> *Try another idea...*

WATER WORKS

What are the best choices then? Well, one cheap solution is to get a filter jug, which removes the bug-busting chlorine element. The carbon filter also takes out some minerals, so another top tip is to change the filter at regular intervals to prevent manky old ones from leaching bacteria back into your drinking water. The jug should be kept in your fridge.

Another option would be to have a filter attached to your tap so that water is continuously filtered or you might want to consider the more expensive, but definitely superior, reverse osmosis systems which separate the water from the other elements that are contained in it. This is what NASA developed for its astronauts (you don't want to think about why they're filtering water!).

> *'Water, water, everywhere,*
> *Nor any drop to drink.'*
> SAMUEL TAYLOR COLERIDGE, *The Rime of the Ancient Mariner*
>
> *Defining idea...*

How did it go?

Q **I drink plenty of tea and coffee so surely I must be getting enough liquid to rehydrate me?**

A *Unfortunately, this isn't going to do it as both tea and coffee are dehydrating. The diuretic effect of these beverages means that they rob the body of more than they supply. I know it's a challenge, but cut down on the amount of tea and coffee you drink. Like everything else, it's just a habit. At first, it will be a struggle but once your body realises how thirsty it is, you'll find that you'll be naturally reaching out for water rather than the colas. The phase where you need to pee more will also pass (excuse the pun), as your body will absorb the water rather than it going right through you. And since it goes through you surprisingly quickly, sipping water rather than glugging huge glasses of the stuff will help. By the way, you'll also begin to like water, rather than expecting what you drink to have flavour!*

Q **What about oral rehydration therapy and isotonic drinks?**

A *Save the oral rehydration therapy (a mixture of salts and sugar) for when you've got cholera – though some people swear by it as a hangover cure! Isotonic drinks are really intended to help athletes absorb water and energy quickly. Some are loaded with sugar – you've been warned!*

12
Allergy or intolerance?

Is it my imagination or is everyone suffering from allergies these days?

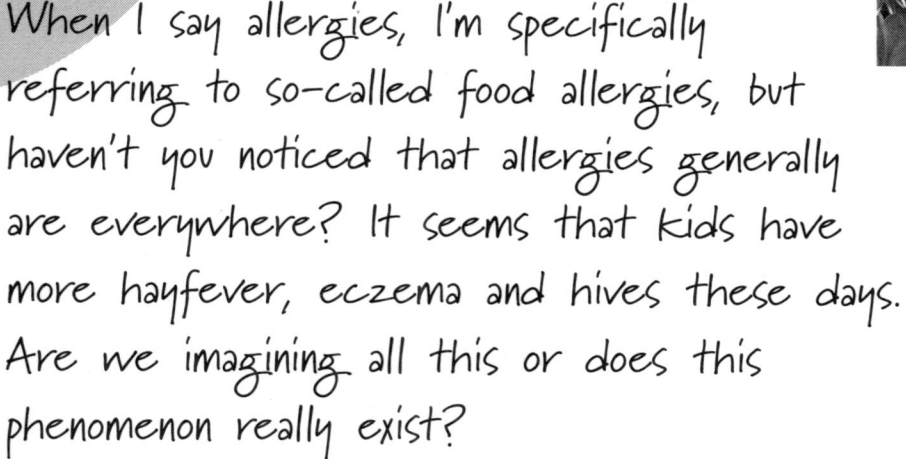

When I say allergies, I'm specifically referring to so-called food allergies, but haven't you noticed that allergies generally are everywhere? It seems that kids have more hayfever, eczema and hives these days. Are we imagining all this or does this phenomenon really exist?

Patrick Holford in his book *The Optimum Nutrition Bible* says that food allergies are affecting close to one in three people. So, perhaps we're not making it up after all. At this point it might be worth defining just what we mean by a food allergy and what we mean by food intolerance, although inevitably opinions differ as to the exact mechanisms of how some reactions to food actually work.

Here's an idea for you... To identify foods that might be having a negative effect on you, keep a food diary for a week. Note down what you eat and when, then examine how you feel afterwards. Look out for feeling down or anxious. Also, your heart may apparently beat faster. Eliminate any suspect foods then replace them with another choice. For example, replace wheat with rye bread. Consider getting in touch with a qualified nutritionist to help you through this process.

Food intolerance is sometimes quite difficult to pin down in that reactions can sometimes occur a long time after the food has been consumed. Symptoms can range from an upset stomach to a general feeling of yeargh or just a foggy, tired, generally below-par sort of feeling. Some experts believe that everyday foods cause a food intolerance to build up. Commonly wheat is seen as a major culprit, but others are gluten, dairy products and eggs. The reasons why certain foods affect us is still under debate in certain circles, but one theory is that larger particles of food, not completely digested by the system, circulate the body causing an inflammatory response that affects our brain chemistry. Another theory is that because we often crave foods that do us the most harm, the body develops an addiction-like response to these foods that act like natural opiates – great when you're having them, but terrible once you experience the inevitable crash that leaves you craving more.

The best way to work out if you might have an intolerance is to avoid a suspect food for four weeks. You might try eliminating wheat, gluten, dairy, mould (e.g. in blue cheeses), chocolate or eggs. You *must* find alternatives to replace the eliminated foods and eliminate them one at a time or you may get pretty hungry. Reintroduce the food after the four weeks is up and pulse test your reaction to it. Consume just

Idea 12 – **Allergy or intolerance?**

that particular food otherwise you won't know what affected your reaction. For example, if you were avoiding eggs, have a large helping of scrambled eggs and take your pulse 15, 30 and 60 minutes before and after. If you're intolerant you'll notice that your pulse will beat significantly faster. Take a note of any other reactions too.

Usually a food allergy is much more immediate. It produces an actual immune response in the body that often manifests itself in hives, rashes, eczema, breathing difficulties, migraine or vomiting. It's normally quite easy to trace the culprit, as a reaction appears very soon after the food has been eaten.

Very severe types of allergy can be life-threatening. A person can die if their reaction to a substance (commonly peanuts) is severe enough for them to go into anaphylactic shock and victims must be taken to hospital immediately. Some sufferers carry around adrenaline shots, which must be administered quickly to avoid lethal consequences.

Try another idea...
You might like to do the detox in IDEA 13, Ready for a detox?

Defining idea...
'One man's food is another man's poison.'
LUCRETIUS

53

How did it go?

Q **I get terribly bloated after eating and this is particularly bad in the evening. Any suggestions?**

A The best thing for you to do is to seek the advice of a qualified nutritionist, but it's also worth avoiding wheat for a week and seeing how you get on. This doesn't mean you starve to death, as there are hundreds of other possible substitutes such as rye, rice or millet. I once had a client who ate Shredded Wheat for breakfast, a sandwich for lunch and pasta for dinner. This isn't a varied diet by any stretch of the imagination. In fact, it's almost a mono diet. Yet the client was quite surprised and convinced that at least her breakfast wasn't wheat! Shredded Wheat? Hmmmm.

Q **How do you avoid food intolerances? Can I stop one developing?**

A The tip here is to eat a wide variety of food. Don't get in a rut. Breakfast is always a tricky one as in a bleary state the same breakfast everyday will be quite appealing. However, try a mixture of yoghurt with nuts and seeds, rye toast, eggs, porridge made with millet and porridge made with oats. Some of my more brave clients even have sardines on toast in the morning.

Q **Is there anything else I should watch for?**

A Again, you can go to a nutritionist to help you identify foods that might be bothering you, but dairy is often a common allergen, especially if you're suffering from mucous problems. Try eating goat or sheep products instead and see how you get on. At the very least, this will ring the changes and make sure that your diet is more varied. There are now lots of alternatives to dairy out there, including rice milk, almond milk and hazelnut milk (never give these milks to infants, as they are not designed to support their nutrition).

13
Ready for a detox?

Detox is such a big buzz word these days, but what exactly does it mean?

In rebellion against the detox diet movement, someone I know did a retox diet during the football season. His method was to drink several pints of lager. The media remind us daily how all the stars have detoxed, but what does this involve?

Doing a detox diet isn't quite as simple as you might think. What detox actually means to you really depends on where you are with your diet now. If you're drinking lots of alcohol, simply eliminating the booze for a few days might constitute a detox diet. To someone who already has quite a pure diet, however, eliminating wheat and dairy might be a detox. Taking stock of where you are is important because if you detox too quickly you could experience a number of unpleasant symptoms, such as headaches, lack of energy and generally feeling unwell. Don't think of doing a detox when you have an important week at work, as you might have a bit of a fuzzy head.

Here's an idea for you...

Get a juicer and start making your own juice. You might like to try a combination of apple and blueberry or carrot and apple. Juices can be full of vitamins and minerals that help the detoxification systems important to the body. But remember to use organic fruit as there are pesticides on conventionally grown fruit.

DON'T MAKE ME

Why should we put ourselves through a detox? Isn't it really hard work? Our bodies are in a constant state of renewal at cell level, but if there's an overload of toxins either from food or environmental sources our bodies struggle to deal with them, effectively putting a strain on the kidneys and liver and taking away energy that could otherwise be used for living. A detox diet allows us to stop overloading the body with harmful substances and, if we give the body plenty of the right nutrients, it can speed up the elimination of toxins and promote cell renewal.

Idea 13 – **Ready for a detox?**

WARM-UP

If you're afraid of becoming Mr or Mrs Fuzzy Potatohead, then the thing to do is to start slowly over a period of one month. Choose in the first week to eliminate coffee, chocolate and caffeine drinks (cola drinks), replacing them with lots of water and herbal teas. In the second week, try eliminating wheat products (cakes, biscuits, pasta) and substitute them with rye bread or other grains such as brown rice, quinoa, buckwheat or millet. In the third week, try substituting dairy products for sheep and goat products. And in the fourth week, increase your water intake up to at least 2 litres (3.5 pints) of water a day, whilst avoiding alcohol.

You might want to take into consideration environmental toxins too and try to avoid them during this period. Are you a smoker? Do you regularly use aerosol sprays? Do you take lots of over-the-counter medication (for example, for headaches)? What about your exposure to traffic fumes? If you're a cyclist, consider wearing a mask to filter fumes.

Try another idea...

You'll find IDEA 6, *Get organic*, IDEA 7, *Superfoods*, and IDEA 34, *Home spa*, essential reading.

Defining idea...

'The world is round and the place which may seem like the end may also be the beginning.'
IVY BAKER PRIEST

57

How did it go?

Q **I want to go a little further with my detoxing. Any suggestions?**

A   Start with the warm-up described above so that when you take it a step further you don't experience unpleasant reactions. Then keep avoiding wheat, alcohol, dairy products and caffeine. Take a week off work if possible and really indulge in your experience. Go shopping and get prepared before you start. You'll need lots of fresh fruit, including lots of lemons, and vegetables. Also, get some vegetable juices (beetroot or carrot are good, but not tomato), millet (an alkaline grain and very detoxifying) and brown rice. If your budget can run to it add in a good antioxidant supplement (advanced antioxidant solgar would be good), some flax seeds and a green superfood (try Kiki's E3 Live or Nature's Living Superfood from www.kiki-health.com). Start your day with a drink of hot water and lemon juice and do some yoga or stretching exercises if possible. Breakfast should be millet porridge made with water, with some fruit and berries added. Intersperse your day with plenty of water and herbal teas. Lunch should be a huge salad that includes many colours – greens, oranges and reds. Dinner should be steamed vegetables and a small portion of brown rice. Before bed, do a breathing exercise. See how wonderful you feel in a week. Take plenty of rest in the first few days – you could get a cleansing reaction where you feel below par, but it will pass.

Q **How often should you detox?**

A   I choose to detox at the beginning of each of the four seasons. Some people use Sundays to do a mini detox where they eat lighter or even do a juice fast where they drink vegetable juice (not tomato) throughout the day and finish with lightly steamed vegetables in the evening.

14
Chemical world

We can't avoid all the man-made chemicals out there. We can, however, choose alternatives for many.

There's no point in getting paranoid. We live in the twenty-first century and there's no going back in time, however much we'd like to! We need to manage the amount of man-made chemicals we draw into our bodies and think of alternatives to those we expose ourselves to daily.

The point is that exposure to low levels of chemicals is relatively harmless. We're surrounded by low-level doses of chemicals, from the fire retardants in our armchairs and mattresses to the toxins in toothpaste and cosmetics. It's the continual exposure to chemicals and the fact that we're so reliant on so many different products that's a worry, say some – the drip, drip, drip. Chemicals are, of course, in everything. Even fruit and vegetables contain chemicals – naturally occurring toxins that protect the plant against attacks by insects, fungi, birds and animals. Day to day these natural chemicals are said to outnumber the man-made ones by a factor of 20,000:1. It has

Here's an idea for you... **Reduce the number of chemicals you are exposed to by purifying the air that you breathe. Air purifiers are available for the home, the car or even to wear when you are out and about. www.healthy-house.co.uk provides these and all sorts of other gizmos for a healthy environment.**

been found that two-thirds of the man-made chemicals are carcinogenic to rats and mice, but so are the natural ones. It seems that although fruit and vegetables might contain toxic elements, they also contain elements that protect us against cancer as well. So, it appears that their toxicity is offset somewhat by the protective factors they provide. Then there's the possibility that we've adapted over millions of years to these natural toxins, whereas we've only been exposed to the man-made ones for the last fifty years or so.

It's tempting to throw the baby out with the bath water forgetting that there have been incidences where chemicals have saved many lives. DDT, for example, helped rid much of the world of the malarial mosquito, although due to its toxicity it's now banned in many countries.

FISH LADY

In the 1960s, some fishermen noticed that something very strange was going on with the fish they caught. Male fish resembled female fish and this led to the discovery of environmental oestrogens (xeno-oestrogens). It's unlikely you'll turn into a fish or from a man into a woman from such low exposure, but it's worth avoiding these sources of xeno-oestrogens wherever possible. Soft plastics are a source, like the plastic wraps for food – it's therefore best to keep cheese in hard plastic airtight containers than wrapped in something like clingfilm. And it isn't good to leave plastic water bottles lying in the sun either.

A QUICK TOUR OF THE NASTIES!

So, what do we mean by man-made chemicals and what do they purportedly do to us?

- **PCBs** (polychlorinated biphenyls) – chemicals that can affect the functioning of the thyroid. They were mainly used as paint additives until they were banned in the 70s, but recent reports show high levels in oily fish.

- **Phthalates** – used to make plastics more flexible, including in children's toys. They're also found in cosmetics. Lab tests have shown that these chemicals affect sperm count and quality.

- **Organotins** – toxic even in small quantities, but are nevertheless found in trainers, mattresses, bed linen, upholstered carpets and floor coverings. These chemicals are known to affect the immune system.

- **Bisphenol A** – found in cosmetics.

- **Tricolosan** – an antibiotic used in some plastic cutting boards and in mouthwashes, detergents, creams and lotions. This chemical is stored in the body for long periods.

Try another idea...

If chemical additives is an area that interests you, check out IDEA 6, *Get organic*.

Defining idea...

'The more clearly we can focus our attention on the wonders and realities of the universe about us, the less taste we shall have for destruction.'
RACHEL CARSON, author of *Silent Spring*, one of the first books that exposed the possible dangers of modern chemicals

How did it go?

Q **This no chemical stuff is all very well, but I don't find the natural alternatives very effective. Any recommendations?**

A   You could try Ecover (www.store.ediblenature.com) for a wonderful selection of nature-friendly products to use in the home. I find them very efficient and changed over to their fabulous washing powder years ago. A network marketing company that has a good reputation for cleaning products is Neways (www.neways.com).

Q **What about cleaning my face? Are there any good products out there?**

A   I use either Dr Hauschka, which is delicious and apparently used by all the top supermodels (www.drhauschka.co.uk), or Jurlique, an Australian company that uses organic and bio-dynamically grown herbs without the use of petro or coal tar chemicals in their products (www.jurlique.com.au).

Q **How can I stop myself from coming into contact with man-made chemicals?**

A   You can't, so stop worrying about it. The trick is not to overexpose yourself to them. If you're cleaning the bathroom with domestic chemicals, make sure the area is well ventilated – open the door and windows and breathe away from the products. After years of being exposed to cleaning fluids, my cleaner is now almost completely allergic to any chemical products, suffering from symptoms such as watering eyes and sneezing. She either has to wear a mask or use natural, non-toxic products. So, avoiding a situation like this before it arises is key!

15
Getting into shape

Weight loss is for life and not just for after Christmas.

The diet industry is worth millions, precisely because diets don't work. If they did, all those diet clubs would be out of business, as the value is in repeaters. Instead of a short-term diet, find a way to eat for life that works yet doesn't make you feel like you're depriving yourself.

The trouble with most diets is that too much organisation, time, concentration and effort is required to count calories or portion sizes. Diets mean that we're thinking about food the whole time, so naturally we eat more or crack under the pressure of it all and have fifty chocolate bars in one hit. In my opinion, the main outmoded theory is calorie counting. Of course, if you eat a tub of lard, which is pure fat, or a deep-fried peanut butter sandwich on white bread with lashings of butter every day then you might put on weight (I had a client who ate this every day before he came

Here's an idea for you...

If you're really determined to lose weight, why not focus on it for a week? Start as you mean to go on and bin unhealthy packages lurking in your cupboards and fridge. Then get hold of the right ingredients: fresh foods and basic dry ingredients like lentils, chickpeas and brown rice. Have a breakfast of porridge with fresh fruit and yoghurt, or eggs on rye toast. For lunch try a great big salad with all the trimmings, but go easy on the dressing – just a little olive oil and lemon juice. End your day with something like grilled fish and broccoli. If you get hungry, a small protein snack will help – nuts and seeds are useful.

to see me!). Part of the equation of weight gain *is* calories in versus calories expended, but this is only part of the jigsaw. Think of all those horrible people who eat exactly what and when they want and never put on an ounce. Don't you just hate them? This proves that something else must be at work.

This something else isn't just one factor, but many. Gut health (including elimination), the level of yeast in your system, how your immune system is functioning and your hormonal health (including that of your thyroid) can all have an effect on your metabolism and how you'll process the food you're eating. Of course, it may be that you're eating all the wrong foods and too much of them, but it might be something else as well and this is best determined by your doctor and with the help of a qualified nutritionist.

OK, enough chat. The bad news is that change is often hard work because it requires you to do something differently. It's that old-fashioned word 'discipline' that freaks people out, but it simply means sticking to a healthy eating plan most of the time, and occasionally when the mood strikes you, going mad.

The trick is to eat foods that will burn slowly and give you sustained energy throughout the day. Ones that burn quickly will rapidly increase your blood sugar levels causing insulin – a hormone that lowers sugar in the blood – to be pumped rapidly into the system. The resulting drop in blood sugar will make you feel drowsy. Things that are white and processed burn quickly (white bread, white rice, potatoes, etc.) – sticks of French bread are like rocket fuel because they turn into sugar very quickly.

While you're at it, check out IDEA 3, *Vital energy*, and IDEA 2, *Digestion up close and personal*.

Try another idea...

Besides lowering the blood sugar, insulin also stores fat, so you may put on weight if your blood sugar is rising and falling like a yo-yo. You need to be eating foods with plenty of fibre in them (such as vegetables), unprocessed grains (brown things), lean protein, essential fats (the clue's in the title) and slow-burning complex carbohydrates. Cutting out stimulants such as tea and coffee in the diet will also help to control the peaks and troughs of blood sugar management. Put simply, don't eat processed foods with highly processed ingredients, which means pretty much anything that comes in a box. Now I think you're ready for the Secret of Life: healthy, unprocessed food tends also to be low-calorie food! There, I said it.

Nearly forgot. Best to get some exercise in too! Apart from the obvious thermodynamic reasons, exercise helps the metabolic functions – breathing, digestion and circulation – to work better. It's like having a powerful car – don't let it rust up in the garage, you need to take it for a spin. Give your body the right fuel and it will run beautifully.

'Physical fitness isn't only one of the most important keys to a healthy body, it is the basis of dynamic and creative intellectual activity.'
JOHN F. KENNEDY

Defining idea...

How did it go?

Q **How do I know if a food is fast or slow burning?**

A *Don't get hung up on this. Basically, protein, non-starchy vegetables and wholegrains (unprocessed grains) are slow burners, and highly processed things such as white bread, fruit juices (think of all that sugar!) and starchy vegetables like potatoes, swede and turnips are relatively speaking faster burners. Obviously, sugar is a no-no.*

Q **I'm used to getting a bit of a lift from coffee and chocolate in the afternoon when I flag. What's wrong with that?**

A *Think of it as being about going the distance rather than being a stop/start sprinter. There's no doubt that a chocolate bar and a sweet coffee will give you a sudden boost in blood sugar and this may jolt you into action, but like so many other highs it'll drop you down again deeper than where you started off. Part of the art of wellbeing is to try to level out those peaks and troughs.*

16
Labelling matters

Have you ever looked at the back of a packet of food and wondered where the actual food was?

The list of ingredients on some packet foods make them look like Martian fodder. Indeed many of the weird and wonderful names certainly aren't things you'd ever use in your home cooking.

Food manufacturers now seem to prefer these long names to the ubiquitous E numbers, as increasingly consumers are realising that E stands for additives.

Food labelling can be hugely confusing. The general rule of thumb is that if the ingredient list barely fits on the back of the packet, put it back on the shelf where you found it. The second rule is that you should recognise the main ingredient and if you don't, or it's something like sugar, reassess your choice. The words 'junk food' should spring to mind.

Here's an idea for you...

Try reading the back of food packets for a week. Don't use items where ingredients aren't in plain English. Watch out especially for hydrogenated fats, which may be cunningly listed as 'shortening'. This is particularly found in cakes, biscuits, margarine and ready meals.

BEWARE THE SUGAR MONSTER!

Sugar is really one to watch as it morphs into all sorts of disguises – glucose, fructose, lactose or maltose and, of course, there's always honey. Watch out too for other forms of sugar like sorbitol, xylitol, mannitol and isomalt. The one that's really crept in is the high fructose corn syrups (sugar dextrose), which isn't the same type of sugar as you find in fruit but is extracted from processing cornstarch to yield glucose. It's much cheaper and sweeter than sugar and is, of course, a firm favourite with food manufacturers – sauces, chewing gum, fruit drinks, canned fruits, dairy products, jams, sweets, bread, bacon and beer are favourite hiding places. Unfortunately, although it may be convenient for the food manufacturers, our bodies struggle to use it as effective fuel and it is easily metabolised as fat. And just as you thought we'd finished with sugar, guess what? There are a whole lot more forms of it, including aspartame (E951), which is 180 times sweeter than sugar. The key ingredients to this are aspartic acid, phenylalanine and methanol, and although the first two are amino acids (protein building blocks) they're not found in this combination in nature.

HOLD BACK ON THE SALT SHAKER

Salt (sodium chloride) is added in generous amounts to processed foods and although we're meant to have a maximum of 1,600 mg (UK guidelines) a day, you can easily exceed this amount if you don't read the labels. Incidentally, if you're

Idea 16 – **Labelling matters**

adding a lot of salt to your food, check your nutrient status because you could be short of zinc. A zinc deficiency can stop your taste buds from performing so well.

Try another idea...

Why not go the other way and check out IDEA 6, *Get organic*, IDEA 7, *Superfoods*, and IDEA 5, *What's in what?*

One good bit of news – a little butter probably beats its synthetic cousin margarine if it contains hydrogenated fats. Fats in this form are very similar to Tupperware, molecularly speaking.

HOW IS YOUR ADDITION?

Food additives are all used for a reason, but there are doubts about their safety. Certainly E284 boric acid has been linked with causing confusion and, interestingly, is also used to eliminate cockroaches and ants. E321 butylated hydroxytoluene (BHT) has been shown to cause haemorrhaging in animals, whilst E220 sulphur dioxide (preservative) can interfere with nutrient absorption and can provoke tingling or flushing. Also, monosodium glutamate (MSG), that favourite additive of Chinese restaurants, is a flavour enhancer that can cause problems in those with sensitivities to it, including headaches and even seizures. But scientists are still undecided about how much of an effect these chemicals exert.

Defining idea...

'*Food is one of life's great pleasures. Shopping for it, preparing and eating it has bound people together for centuries. It is in eating together that we are socialised. In the end it's about what kind of society we want.*'
FELICITY LAWRENCE, author of *Not on the Label*, an exposé of the food industry.

How did it go?

Q **I always go for the low-fat options as I'm quite health conscious. Yoghurts are my particular favourite. Are these OK?**

A   Although the yoghurt may be low fat, it might be high in sugar – some small single-portion yoghurts contain at least four teaspoons of the stuff. Another ingredient to watch out for in yoghurts is modified starch, which is derived from corn and used as a cheap filling agent and thickener. It attracts water, thus adding bulk. Further, to make your banana yoghurt yellow, colourings are often added. And just one more thing to watch out for – if it's labelled 'strawberry yoghurt' it must have some real fruit content, but if it says 'strawberry-flavoured yoghurt' you have just entered synthetic city.

Q **Although my little boy has a lovely nature, sometimes he goes nuts, gets agitated, rude and can't sit still. Is it something he's eating or am I imagining food can have this effect?**

A   It's probably not your imagination at all. E102 tartrazine has been linked with hyperactivity in children and it's found in orange colourings.

Idea 16 – **Labelling matters**

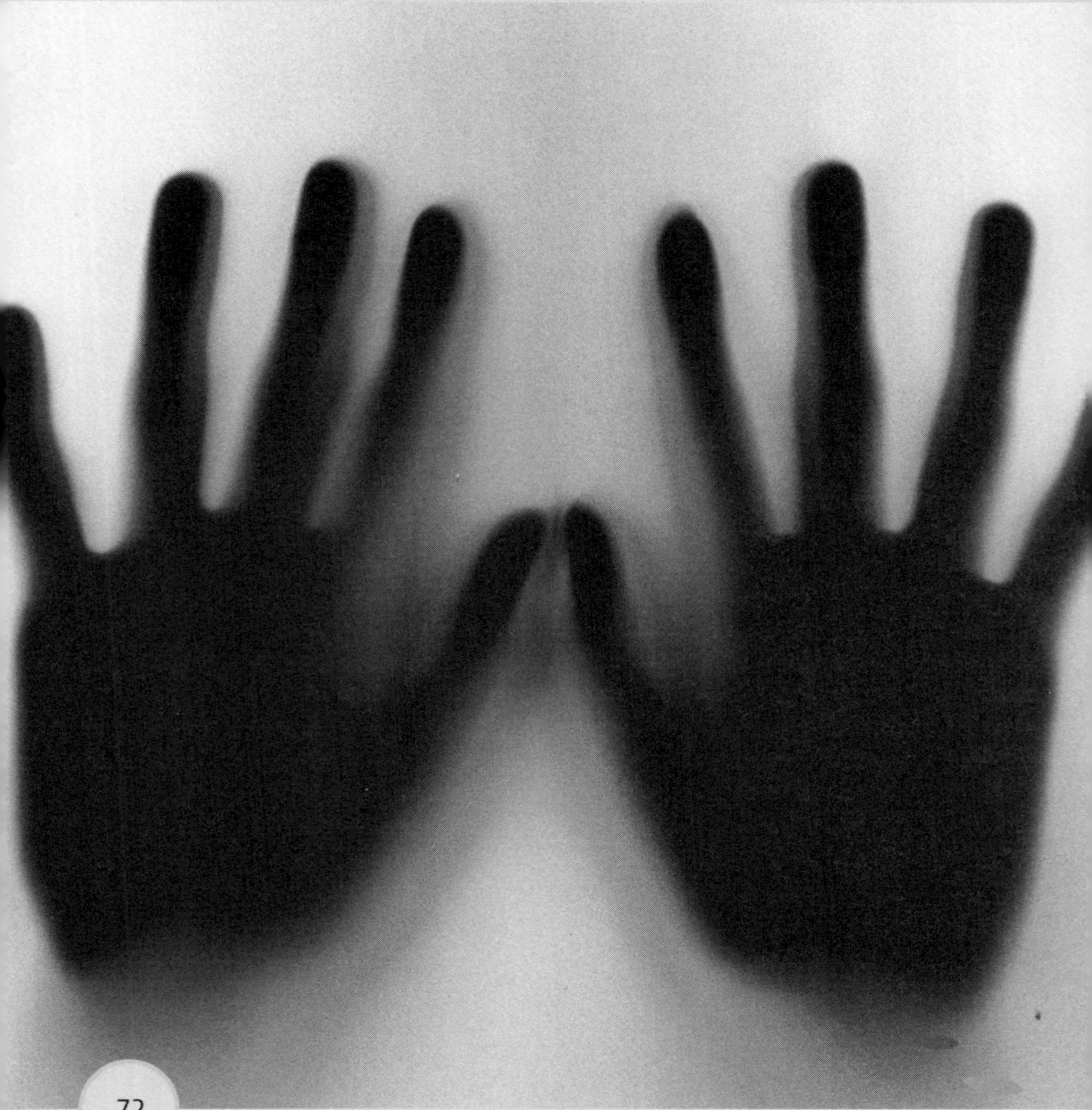

17

Get your nutritional act together

You've made the brilliant decision to take your health and nutrition into your own hands. Now what?

Put some solid systems in place to ensure that your good intentions actually get done. There's nothing more stressful than hundreds of 'I shoulds' running loose in your brain, like 'I really should buy fresh stuff instead of ready meals.'

My first tip is to write all these Shoulds down somewhere so that you can quit worrying about them. Break your Shoulds into sections, such as Diet Shoulds, Exercise Shoulds and Stress-busting Shoulds. Give each Should a priority rating from one to three and tackle the high scorers first. So, if 'I should stop having nine cups of coffee a day' is more of a priority than 'I should stop eating that extra square of chocolate a day', score it as a three and make it something you'll tackle this month. Only aim to take on three Shoulds a month – too many and you won't do them. Get the high-scoring ones under your belt before you take on the lower scorers.

Here's an idea for you...

First go through your cupboards and throw out everything with unrecognisable ingredients on the back of the pack. The general rule is get rid of any ingredient that comprises more than three syllables as this usually means that it's a chemical ingredient that might not be a healthy option. You don't have to actually throw food away, just give it to less healthy friends who don't care that the ingredients are in a kind of chemical Greek.

Choose a day to start the healthy new you, but don't make it a Monday as it's always too depressing to start something at the beginning of the week, especially as the weekend is so far away. Take just one month at a time and say to yourself you'll stick to it for that month. In this way, you won't feel that what you're going to do will be forever. If you think that something is forever, you tend to rebel against it and are less likely to stick to it.

Once you've got rid of all the old packets of food that are lurking around in your cupboards, it's time to go shopping for the basics. You'll need some of the following essential cupboard starters to get you going:

- Organic porridge oats and millet
- Rice milk – just for a change!
- Brown rice, quinoa (a wacky kind of grain) and wheat-free pasta
- Almonds, brazil nuts and cashew nuts
- Pumpkin seeds and sunflower seeds
- Oatcakes and rice cakes
- Tahini and houmous

Idea 17 – **Get your nutritional act together**

- Extra virgin olive oil
- Tuna in olive oil
- Lentils and chickpeas
- Tinned tomatoes, sweetcorn, butterbeans and artichoke hearts
- Dried herbs, pepper, tamari (a kind of wheat-free soya sauce), olives, pesto, bragg liquid aminos (a bit like soya sauce)

> **Try another idea...**
>
> Have a look at IDEA 44, *You're the most important person in your life* and IDEA 47, *Daily habits*. And if you're stressed you're not going to get your act together, so read IDEA 4, *Stressed out*.

These are only suggestions, of course. You'll probably want to add other stuff and take away anything you don't like.

Also, load the fridge with plenty of fresh vegetables. Ones that keep are broccoli, cauliflower, red cabbage and cabbage. Frozen vegetables can be useful too, so get some peas and spinach in.

I once had a client who asked me why I'd put tuna in olive oil on the list. This is simply because I really hate tuna in brine, which I think tastes like dry old bits of wood. But hey, each to his own! If you like tuna in brine or are worried about the extra calories the oil will add, then brine it is. Likewise, anchovies. If there's one thing I detest it's anchovies, but if you like them then by all means add them to your cupboard basics.

> **Defining idea...**
>
> *'Be prepared.'*
> SCOUTING MOTTO, if you have all you need in place, then your changes will stick!

75

How did it go?

Q **My intentions are great, but I find that because I'm working such long hours I never seem to have the time to go shopping to get good food in. How can I make the changes necessary for my new healthy life?**

A   *Obvious one this, but take a good hard look at your 'life/work' balance. I hate this phrase, but it seems to sum things up here. Your life is seriously out of balance if on a daily basis you're unable to achieve even your basic shopping. You could get in touch with Coach U (www.coachu.com; www.findacoach.com) who might be able to help you locate a life coach to sort you out.*

Q **Usually I go at a new regime like a bull in a china shop and change everything in a week, but by week two everything has fallen by the wayside. Any tips to avoid this?**

A   *First of all, never be ashamed if you fall off the nutrition/health horse. It doesn't matter how many times you fall off, just so long as you keep jumping back on again! Those that don't climb back on fail. So, if you mess up, just start again. Tomorrow is a new day!*

The other thing to do is build on your habits. A great website is Dr Andrew Weil's site at www.myoptimumhealthplan.com. He encourages small changes daily and has great recipes and ideas for exercise. Check it out as it's really, really good!

18
What does a day look like?

It's a wonder we eat anything at all considering the masses of conflicting information regarding food and diet. How can we come out of this mire of information with a sensible eating programme?

Given farming scandals ranging from battery chickens to mad cows, wouldn't it be much easier to take a whole load of vitamin pills and stuff them down our throats like they do on space stations?

In a way, choosing what to eat isn't rocket science. We all know in our heart of hearts that eating high-fat, high-sugar foods can't be good for us. Yet it's so darned tasty, isn't it? There are enough government campaigns to improve health for us to know what we should be eating. In Britain, the government has been looking at a way to implement a fat tax on junk food in order to bring under control an explosion in child obesity and it's considering banning vending machines selling rubbish food in schools. If you think that a can of cola contains 30 g of sugar or the equivalent in corn syrup, it's no wonder our kids are contesting for the title of Fattest Kids on Earth.

Here's an idea for you... For a week try to have a different breakfast every day. You could include different types of grains such as millet and quinoa. Some clients of mine even have mackerel on toast!

When producing a food product, the manufacturer is trying to add value to a plain ingredient (for example, flour) by making it into something that has a high perceived value, in other words something for which you would pay a lot more money for than the original raw material. Manufacturers also need to add ingredients that will preserve the food and stop it being a danger to the public. The food scientists add other ingredients, some for measures of public safety and some for economic reasons, perhaps to give the food a long shelf life so that distribution is easier. This is how ingredients like trans-fats or hydrogen-hardened fat, used a lot in baked goods, manage to creep into our food chain. The Food Standards Agency in the UK says, 'Trans-fats have no nutritional benefits and because of the effects they have on blood cholesterol they increase the risk of coronary heart disease…evidence suggests that the adverse effects of trans-fats are worse than saturated fats.'

So where does that all leave us? Quite simply, buy and cook the ingredients yourself! I know you're thinking that you can't possibly afford the time this might take. However, in my opinion you can't possibly afford not to find the time. Start investing in your health immediately! I'm now going to take you through a really easy-to-do day, which will balance your blood sugar, stop cravings and take less time to do than opening a ready meal. I promise.

Idea 18 - **What does a day look like?**

I bet your mum always told you that the most important meal in the day was breakfast. She would be right. Have something like porridge oats (oatmeal) – the thick, chunky-looking fellows, not what I call the hamster-bedding type. Shove two handfuls in a bowl then add some organic milk, rice milk or nut milk (like almond or hazelnut). Here's the trick – you don't have to actually cook it into porridge, just soak the oats in the milk for a few minutes then add some chopped fruit and nuts. The very worthy should add some flax seeds on top of all this as they're great for the digestive system.

Lunch could be a big, juicy salad, soup or a baked potato with cottage cheese. Although it would obviously be much better if you make it yourself, you could buy this at your local lunch venue. Lunch is often the most difficult meal to achieve because you'll try to source it from around work. If you get stuck then cook more the night before and bring the remainder in the next day.

Dinner is easy as you largely control this yourself. It could be an organic salmon steak with steamed vegetables and sweet potatoes, or a stir-fry, or a lentil or chickpea recipe – the choices are endless. It really doesn't take long to stick a piece of chicken under the grill and steam some vegetables. Look at pictures in cookbooks for inspiration, without actually following a recipe to the letter, which is boring unless you're really into cooking. Great cookbooks include *The Optimum Nutrition Cookbook* by Patrick Holford and *The Healthy Kitchen* by Andrew Weil.

For more about food and diet, why not look at IDEA 15, *Getting into shape*, and IDEA 17, *Get your nutritional act together*.

Try another idea...

'Variety is the spice of life.'
Take note of this saying and vary your daily routine as much as you can!

Defining idea...

79

How did it go?

Q **Everyone tells me breakfast is the most important meal, but I don't have the time so I find myself having 'deskfast', which usually consists of one of those breakfast bars. Can you name an alternative that's both fast and good?**

A   *I bet you find you have the time to make a coffee before you leave home. If so, then you have the time to make a smoothie. Try throwing half a banana into the blender along with a half pint of skimmed milk and a couple of handfuls of frozen fruits or berries. Hit the button and you have an icy protein/energy/vitamin drink.*

Q **Lunchtime for me either means sandwiches or the fast food over the road. Any suggestions?**

A   *Even fast-food outlets are bowing to the pressure to offer healthy options, including salads and 'wraps'. If the one opposite your workplace doesn't then try asking them to. Repeatedly. When it comes to sandwiches, try to think about what you choose. Is there a whole bread alternative? Could you skip bacon and replace it (from time to time) with roast vegetables, houmus or skinless chicken?*

19

Ageing gracefully

We live in a youth culture, but the oldies are fighting back!

There are some great role models of the older person done good. Just look at Joan Collins who can 'pull' a man who is generations younger than her, and Mick Jagger who can still shake his bootie with the best of his younger fans and girlfriends.

Perfection comes at a high cost though, both in financial and maintenance terms. Plastic surgery, once a last resort, is becoming commonplace with a nip and a tuck here, there and everywhere. Never a fan myself, I was almost converted when I saw TV personality Anne Robinson. Still, there has to be an easier way, and perhaps the best thing to do is to start preventative measures early enough.

Here's an idea for you...

If you can't give up smoking, the next best thing is to take antioxidant vitamins and minerals – Solgar's advanced antioxidant is a good formula. Allen Carr is apparently the man you need to quit the weed (www.allencarrseasyway.com). Giving up the easy way is his mantra, so why not give it a try?

In terms of the ageing process, free radicals are public enemy number one. Free radicals are a by-product of oxygen metabolism and are mopped up by certain vitamins in the body plus the body's own amazing enzymes. Free-radical activity is intensified by modern living – environmental pollution, stress, drinking, smoking. The heroes of the story are the antioxidant vitamins and minerals that are crusading against these naughty oxidising elements and sacrificing themselves in order to save you, especially vitamins C and E, betacarotene and selenium. And where can you find more of these superheroes? I'm sure you've guessed it already. From your food. Betacarotene and vitamin C are derived mainly from fresh fruit and vegetables – the brighter the colour and the more varied the better. Vitamin C is found in citrus fruit, berries, peppers, potatoes and tomatoes; vitamin E is found in wheat germ, nuts and leafy green vegetables; and selenium can be found in fish, asparagus and the humble Brazil nut.

Idea 19 - **Ageing gracefully**

STUFFED FULL OF FRUIT

Even the government encourages us to eat five portions of fruit and vegetables a day, so at least get into the habit of having fruit around you – ask at work if you can have a fruit bowl for the workers (often quite a cheap way to make the workforce feel appreciated). Try to avoid environmental pollution where you can, without becoming paranoid about it. For example, if you do a lot of city cycling consider a mask with a carbon filter. Smoking is one of the quickest ways to dry up the fountain of youth. It steals your vitamins because it sets off a chain of free radical damage, so giving up is the best thing to do. Limit drinking to three times a week so that your liver – your pollution-processing organ – gets a wee holiday. And make sure that you're not exposing yourself to too many household chemicals. Get the nonchemical versions – they do work, honest! (Try Ecover products, which aren't so harsh on the environment.) Lastly, think about the chemicals you're drawing into yourself in the form of perfumes, deodorants and cosmetics and go for more natural alternatives such as PitRok deodorant (www.pitrok.co.uk).

Check out IDEA 11, *Water babies*, IDEA 7, *Superfoods*, and IDEA 27, *Take a walk on the wild side*.

Try another idea...

'Age before beauty.'
With age comes wisdom. Who'd really want to be nineteen again? OK, you're right, I would

Defining idea...

83

How did it go?

Q **I don't want to be one of those old ladies who limp along with a zimmer frame. Any tips for avoiding stiffness in old age?**

A Luckily you can do masses right now. First: move it, don't lose it – keep flexible by doing stretching exercises. Yoga is good for this, but you don't have to contort yourself into any funny positions to get value! Gently does it. Doing some weight-bearing exercise will help protect your bone density, but this can simply be walking for half an hour each day. Take your fish oils, but make sure they're pure. Other joint formulas, like MSM and glucosamine, are also available.

Q **Do you have any other tips to keep the fountain of youth bubbling away?**

A Not directly related to nutrition, but it's really important to keep your thinking flexible as well as your body. Old age is when someone asks you to a party and you say no because you don't want to miss the next episode of your favourite soap. Old age is when you start saying no instead of yes.

Q **What could I do every day towards warding off the wrinkles?**

A Don't get dehydrated. Older people are less able to conserve water through the kidneys plus they have a significantly lower thirst sensation. So, get into the habit now of drinking water. At first it might feel like an effort, but pretty soon you'll wonder what on earth you were playing at before! Remember that sipping hydrates the cells, whereas gulping will leave you wanting to go to the loo all the time!

20

Nutrition: the basics

There are so many different diets and ways of eating that it's no wonder we're thoroughly confused. Here's a balanced view of the basics of good nutrition.

aloe vera

One minute vitamin C is good for you, the next it's causing cancer. We all change to margarine, then lo and behold we're told to change back to butter. Let's try to make sense of it all.

The food we eat can be divided up into three major 'macro' nutrient groups: carbohydrates, proteins and fats.

CURB THE CARBS?

The body uses carbohydrates (carbs) as its main fuel. Carbs can be divided into two types: 'fast burning' (junk food, processed food, honey, sweet foods) and 'slow burning' (whole grains, fresh fruit and veg grains). The type of carbs you should

85

Here's an idea for you... **Up the amount of vegetarian protein in your diet – try tofu, lentils and grains such as quinoa. If you can't be bothered to cook lentils, get an organic brand in a tin (cheating I know). Mix them with tomatoes, olives, cucumber and feta cheese – nice and easy.**

curb is the fast-burning carbs because these will give you a surge of energy followed by a nasty crash. And avoid rocket-fuel carbohydrates such as white bread, white rice, cakes, biscuits and sugar. Slow-burning complex carbohydrates, however, should make up about 70% of your diet. These tend to be complex carbohydrates and usually have more fibre in them to slow down the way sugar is released into your system.

PERFECT PROTEIN

Protein contains the building blocks (amino acids) that are used for making enzymes, hormones, antibodies and neurotransmitters as well as for repair of the body and for growth. Protein isn't just about huge slabs of juicy steak. Vegetarian sources of protein are important to consider and include beans, tofu, quinoa (a type of grain) and lentils. You should be aiming to get about 15% of your calories through protein, so aim to eat plenty of vegetarian sources, which are less acid forming, and also consider some cheese and eggs, but not in excess. If you eat meat, have it no more than three times a week.

Idea 20 – **Nutrition: the basics**

FEAR OF FAT

A fear of fat has been drummed into us. Yet it's only the wrong kind of fat we should be scared of, not good fats. There are two main types of fat: saturated fats (hard fat) and unsaturated fats. Saturated fats are not essential for the body to function. There are also two main categories of unsaturated fats: monounsaturated (olive oil is in this group) and polyunsaturated. Some polyunsaturated fats are good for your brain and generally make the body work efficiently. In fact, they're known as essential fatty acids (EFAs) – the name speaks for itself. EFAs are destroyed by heat and light so, despite some manufacturers' health claims, the benefits of these fats are likely to have been destroyed once foods are processed. You should aim to get about 15% of your calories through good-quality EFAs. Each day, supplement a pure fish oil or flax seed oil, and eat plenty of nuts and seeds. And avoid too many saturated fats or the type of fats found in processed foods.

Try another idea...

If you found this interesting, have a look at IDEA 1, *What goes in must come out*, IDEA 2, *Digestion up close and personal*, and IDEA 8, *Eat fat.*

Defining idea...

'Any healthy man can go without food for two days – but not without poetry.'
CHARLES BAUDELAIRE

87

How did it go?

Q **Proper nutrition is all very well, but I don't really have time to shop and cook. How can I get round this?**

A *Hmmm. I don't think you can get round it entirely! If you look at a convenience food label, you'll realise that you don't recognise half the ingredients, and personally, I'd rather eat stuff I've at least heard of! So buy some 'real' food. This isn't difficult. You can buy fish or chicken for the week and freeze it, remembering to take it out before you go to work. Stock the fridge with vegetables that don't go off quickly like broccoli, cabbage and red cabbage and get some frozen peas. Then when you get home, stick the fish or chicken under the grill and steam some vegetables in a steamer. Quicker than opening those packets!*

Q **What about all the fuss in the press about the low-carbohydrate and high-protein diets? My friend lost loads of weight. Should I try it?**

A *Yes, if you want to lose friends by having stinky breath! (Halitosis is a side effect of these diets.) The theory in a nutshell is that if carbohydrates aren't burned by the body as energy, then they're deposited as fat and if you give the body protein and fat, the body won't deposit fat so easily. Read the book (Dr Atkins New Diet Revolution by Dr Robert C. Atkins) to get his side of the story! There are several flaws with this kind of diet, not least having to eat so much meat, which is full of saturated fat – and we all know what that does to the heart and arteries! By eating a healthy diet, you'll lose weight naturally and keep it off!*

21
Out there and doing it

I hate the gym. So, what are the alternatives?

I hate the music in gyms. I hate the smell of them. I don't like the machines and they don't like me. I only have to attempt to trot on the treadmill and I find myself getting spat off like Wile E. Coyote in another failed attempt to catch the Roadrunner!

I just don't think the gym is beautiful. And, on top of that, no one talks to each other because they're so busy doing exercise. OK, I know that's what you're supposed to be doing, but still. It's all those mirrors, too. Everyone is so busy being narcissistic and it's so dehumanising – loud music, bright lights, functional, high speed. You're in and out of there with no connection to the rest of the human race. The other obvious thing wrong with the gym is that you join up and then don't go for a whole year. When you finally do go, out of guilt, you spend a wad of cash in accumulated membership fees on one swim. Sorry, I'll stop ranting, but did I mention that I don't like the gym?

> **Here's an idea for you...**
>
> Exercising at home is another way to avoid the gym. Why not check out psychocalisthenics (www.pcals.com)? This is a form of exercise that revitalises your whole system yet takes just 15 minutes to do.

GETTING IT WHERE YOU CAN

So, what other possibilities are there? Go and exercise outside. You don't have to be in the midst of the glorious countryside for this one. Your local park will do. Use the park benches to stretch, use steps to run up and use lampposts as distance markers. Let your imagination run wild as to what you can use in the environment to help you in your mission (no gym fitness). Set goals – a good one might be to count the number of times you run round the park, each time trying to improve upon the last. I have a great little run that I do by the River Thames in London (down by Chelsea Harbour) where you can see loads of wildlife, cranes, fish, swans and ducks, despite being in the city. What a pleasure.

Getting some aerobic exercise by running and walking will obviously increase your cardiovascular fitness, and even in the city (away from busy roads) you'll benefit from breathing 'fresh' air into your lungs. Pumping your heart muscle is important to get your lymph system moving – your lymph has no internal pump. The benefit of aerobic exercise is that it is thought to protect you against all sorts of nasty diseases, including some types of cancers and heart disease, plus it makes your bones stronger. So, get out there and do some cardiovascular stuff. Run, jog or walk for at least 20 minutes each day.

Idea 21 - **Out there and doing it**

- **Power walking** – Stride out when you walk. Get into it by loading your iPod up with some seriously good music.

- **Jump higher** – Skipping is a wonderful way to get your ticker really going. Apparently, jumping rope has the calorie-burning capacity of jogging for one mile. But you have to really go for it – no weedy jumping allowed.

- **Warm up and wind down** – Don't forget to stretch at the beginning and end of your workouts. Warm, stretched muscles are muscles that are less likely to be injured.

Try another idea...

For more on exercise away from the gym look at IDEA 27, *Take a walk on the wild side*, IDEA 31, *Get on yer bike* and IDEA 33, *Games other people play*. Also see IDEA 22, *Have a heart (rate monitor)*.

Defining idea...

'I am at two with nature.'
WOODY ALLEN

91

How did it go?

Q **How can I make sure I actually get my kit on and make it out the door?**

A   I bribe myself. I have a little tick chart pinned on the fridge with my exercise schedule listed out. Two runs, two walks, yoga and swimming. Once I've accomplished a month with no passes, I'm allowed a treat (my favourite being a massage). If I mess up even once during the month, no treat.

Q **I'm getting bored of doing the same old circuit. Any tips?**

A   Me too, but what I try to do is reverse the circuit and go round the other way, or at weekends I do a longer walk/run and usually make sure that I go to a new area. Don't get stuck in your own neighbourhood. Ring up friends in other areas and plan to walk/run with them where they live. By ringing the changes, when you return to your own circuit it won't seem so boring.

Idea 21 – **Out there and doing it**

52 Brilliant Ideas – **Get healthy for good**

22
Have a heart (rate monitor)

Do you hate jogging/running? All that wobbly flesh jigging up and down?

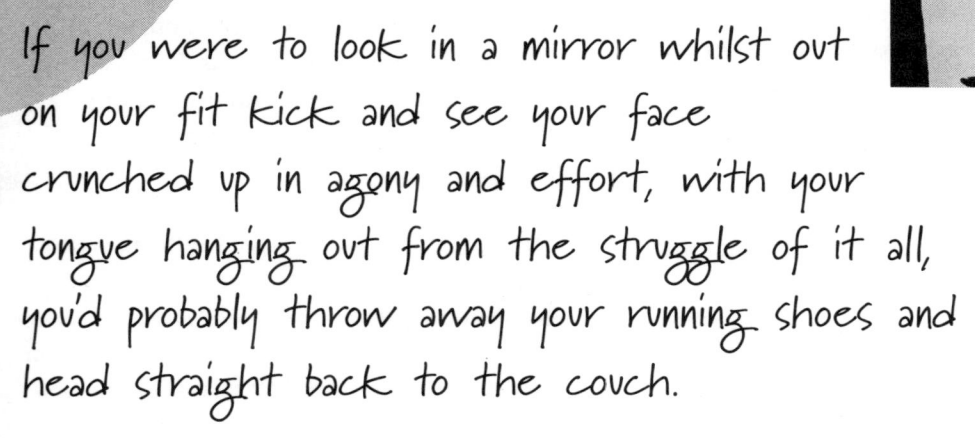

If you were to look in a mirror whilst out on your fit kick and see your face crunched up in agony and effort, with your tongue hanging out from the struggle of it all, you'd probably throw away your running shoes and head straight back to the couch.

Well, that's how I was until I had my Pauline conversion. You simply have to get a heart rate monitor. Now! No excuses. In my experience, this is the only way to attempt running without knackering yourself in the process. You exercise according to your own fitness level and don't try to race ahead before you're ready. You could buy a heart rate monitor from www.polarusa.com or www.heartratemonitor.co.uk or any good sports shop. Some gyms also sell them.

Brilliant Ideas – **Get healthy for good**

Here's an idea for you...

Try these two fabulous books that teach you how to exercise with heart rate monitors: *The Maffetone Method* **by Dr Philip Maffetone and** *Slow Burn* **by Stu Mittleman. Also, if you really get into this you could get a monitor that allows you to set zones. An alarm will then sing out as soon as you stray from the selected zone. In other words, your watch will tick you off if you start to slack off or put your foot to the floor with a little too much gusto.**

Defining idea...

'Mind is everything, muscles mere pieces of rubber. All that I am, I am because of my mind.'
PAAVO NURMI, nine-time Olympic gold medalist.

A heart rate monitor usually has two parts: a chest strap and a sports watch. The strap picks up your heartbeat, which is displayed on the watch. In this way you can tell if your training is too strenuous or not strenuous enough. A few years back, I decided to wear my new heart rate monitor around the house whilst I performed a few domestic tasks. I realised my fitness needed serious attention when my heart rate, whilst peeling a carrot, was up through the roof!

Don't go for the all-singing, all-dancing version of the heart rate monitor to start with. There are versions that will tell you how many calories you've burned, how far you've been on your training and record all sorts of things you might want to forget. If you're new to heart rate monitors then just buy a basic model like a Polar A3. You can always trade up later if you get into it. As you can imagine, there are hundreds of models catering for various fitness audiences.

Idea 22 – **Have a heart (rate monitor)**

WALK THE WALK

Walking is a great way to get started. It's the safest work-out. We all know how to do it for starters! The intensity is low but it's great for burning fat. Walking is also a great de-stressor and doesn't require any expensive gear, just put on your heart rate monitor and a pair of trainers and hit the road. If you do decide to get into running in a serious way, you might consider an assessment with a physiotherapist who will let you know what type of stretching and other exercise would be good for you. In your hurry to get fit, it's always worth making sure that you aren't overstraining yourself in any way. A big one to watch out for is your knee health. Even taking a couple of lessons in running from a well-qualified personal trainer might save you money in the end by getting your running style right from the outset.

A heart rate monitor will:

- help you moderate your exercise intensity;
- help motivate you.
- accurately measure your heart rate; and
- enable you to judge improvement over time, like having your own personal trainer.

You might also want to look at IDEA 30, *Human racing*, and set yourself the challenge of an event.

Try another idea...

'Run like hell and get the agony over with.'
CLARENCE DEMAR, professional linotyper, writer, Sunday school teacher, boy scout master, farmer – and seven-times winner of the Boston marathon.

Defining idea...

97

How did it go?

Q How do I know what the right level of training is for me? What should my heart rate be?

A I'm glad you asked that. There are different formulae for calculating your heart rate, but presuming you're not about to train to be an Olympic sprinter go with Maffetone's 'aerobic' maximum rate, by which your optimal heart rate for aerobic training is determined by the 180 formula: your age subtracted from 180. This is fine if you've been exercising regularly (four times a week) for two years without any problems. However, if you're recovering from a major illness or on medication subtract 10 (if this applies to you, check with a doctor before you start exercising); if you've not exercised before, if exercise has been patchy, you get loads of colds or have allergies or asthma, subtract 5; if you're a competitive athlete and have been training for two years without any problems or injury, then add 5. You will then have your maximum aerobic heart rate. Your every-day training zone will then range from that number to 10 beats below that number. For example, if your maximum heartbeat is 155 then your training zone would be 145 to 155. (Thanks to Dr Philip Maffetone for this formula.)

Q Hang on a minute, my heart-rate formula is always the same. Does that mean I'm not improving?

A This is the cunning bit. As your fitness improves, your heat beat slows down, so you have to work harder to maintain the same heart rate.

23

Gotta run

Run for your health, social life, waistline or sanity. There are as many reasons to run as there are runners and if you get out there and find your own perfect pace you'll never look back.

A run. A jog. A shambolic shuffle. Never mind your style or speed, the fact remains that as bipeds we were pretty much made for this running malarkey.

It's relatively cheap (though you should look to spend as much as you can afford on decent shoes and a good sports bra) and anyone can do it pretty much anywhere (though with greater and lesser degrees of pleasure). It's still about the best calorie-burning exercise known to man and it builds up bone density, endurance, toned thighs and stronger heart and lungs. More than that though, for many of us it can be a special time, a quiet time set aside for thinking things over or perhaps *not* thinking things over.

Defining idea...

'You really just can't beat the outdoors. You get to see other runners and there's always somewhere to spit. My favourite time to run is about five o'clock at night so I'm moving faster than all the sad commuters stuck in their cars. It makes me glad to be alive, even when it's raining.'
DRAGON BREATH, one of the runners in the *Runners World* online community.

Here's an idea for you...

Having a running partner can make all the difference. It can make time fly as you chat, turn a fitness effort into 'quality time' with friends or family and it can help motivate you to show up in the first place. Look online and in local papers for running clubs. Many gyms also have groups of runners and they'll often be happy for newcomers to join regardless of whether or not you're a member.

Most runners talk about feelings of enhanced self-esteem and, while it may be tiresome to listen to, you can't help but notice the self-satisfaction, even smugness, of the hardcore harrier. Some people reach the point where if they can't run they feel out of sorts. So, what's holding you back?

For many, it's the fear that we just can't do it. So, take it one step at a time (so to speak). I know a man called Luke Cunningham who found he wasn't so keen on what he saw in the mirror and decided to try jogging. He started by running for a few minutes, stopping to catch his breath and then running back. And he still talks of the sense of satisfaction from running over seven minutes each way – a full quarter of an hour of running. Luke now competes in seven-day events over hundreds of kilometres of desert.

Just take it at your own pace and plan where you will run. Take enough money to buy a bus ticket back in case you get tired or sprain something. Know where you are going and where you will find water, such as a drinking fountain, a café or from a bottle you take with you. Try not to have to cross roads (it's easy for your attention to wander at crucial moments) or run past potential stress factors such as a corner where the local kids hang out or where there's a territorial aggressive dog. Don't forget to think about the weather – runners suffer sunburn too and if there's any wind it's always easier to set out against the wind and run back with it behind you.

Try another idea...

Why not try a race? See IDEA 30, *Human racing*.

Idea 23 – **Gotta run**

Q **I run on a treadmill at the gym. Why would I go outside?**

A If you can keep going with nothing to distract you but the mirror and MTV, then good luck to you. For some, however, fresh air is priority and they find it far easier to keep going when distracted by passers-by, scenery and other runners. If you feel self-conscious, try running with a mate. If you don't have a running mate then head for a park where you'll find a wide range of other joggers just like you.

Q **Everyone mentions good shoes. What exactly are good shoes?**

A It depends on a whole host of factors such as the type of run you do, the way your foot strikes the ground as you run, the shape of your arches and your weight. Get it right and the shoe will cushion you where your foot hits the floor and help you roll across your foot and spring into the next stride. Get it wrong and in the long term you risk discomfort and even injuries. The best thing to do is to find a seriously good shoe shop (specialised running shops usually advertise themselves as such in magazines and online). Take your old shoes along with you to show them the wear pattern and never trust a salesperson who doesn't want to see you run in the shoes you try out. At least one shop I know insists on videoing your feet as you run on a treadmill and analysing your footstrike and gait. Nor does that attention to detail mean that you end up paying more. Personally I've never found specialists trying to upsell me to the latest trendy model. I can't say the same for general sports shops.

How did it go?

52 Brilliant Ideas – **Get healthy for good**

24
Geeing up for the gym

However much you might hate the idea of the gym, it can prove to be extremely effective and convenient in terms of your fitness goals and it doesn't have to be boring.

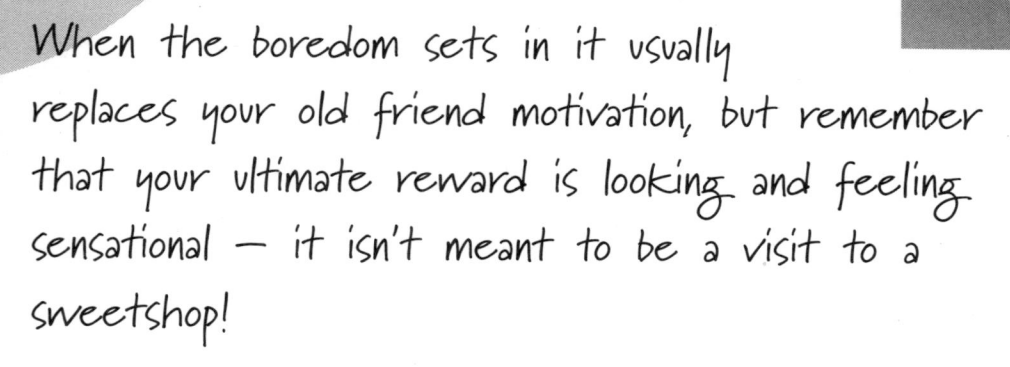

When the boredom sets in it usually replaces your old friend motivation, but remember that your ultimate reward is looking and feeling sensational — it isn't meant to be a visit to a sweetshop!

Most gyms have a good range of classes ranging from yoga, Pilates, kick-boxing and circuit training to dance classes, spinning (a work-out on a stationary bike), and running and rowing clubs. Find some classes that suit you, and then simply enjoy them!

WHICH GYM?

Find a gym that you'll actually go to in order to keep excuses like it not being on your way to/from work at bay. Your motto should be: Location, Location, Location!

Here's an idea for you...

Get the right kit. You'll feel like you're taking the whole thing seriously and having spent the money you'll have to turn up! Supportive, breathable shoes are a must. Find a reputable sports store that can advise you on the best shoes for your activity. Or buy online. Wear an outfit that you'll be comfortable in. You don't have to go clad in Lycra. If you feel better in shorts or jogging pants/leggings then fine, but ensure that whatever you choose allows for a good range of movement.

...and another

Women: ensure that your bra offers good support for your chosen activity. See www.lessbounce.com.

WHAT TO DO?

Most gyms will provide an induction and possibly a session with a trainer – make use of this. Decide on your goal and why you're there. Is it for weight loss, for weight gain, to train for an event, to improve fitness or to build strength? Whatever your reason, inform your trainer so they can design a programme specifically aimed at you and your needs. What about considering a personal trainer, even if you do it just once a month?

INCLUDE WEIGHT-TRAINING

Weight training doesn't mean you'll end up looking like Arnie. It's a great way to add tone and definition to your body and will increase lean muscle mass, thus help to manage weight. Using weights has the added bonus of strengthening your bones. Change your technique from time to time. Challenge your body and do super-slow repetitions or try doing three or four sets back to back with just a 10-second rest in between (leave this for when you're a little more advanced).

Idea 24 – Geeing up for the gym

Try these:

Circuit training
This can be done in a class or you can make up your own. Keep moving from machine to machine and include free-weights and some abdominal work.

Core stability
A very important factor in overall strength, this engages the stabilising muscles and initially may feel like you're not working very hard. Take part in a class or have a trainer show you how to use the gym balls. Building up core stability can help prevent injuries and improve posture. It's a departure from just giving it welly on all the machines.

Low intensity
Include this as a great way to improve stamina and to add some variety.

And above all:

Focus!
Don't just plonk yourself on the exercise bike with your favourite weekly. Find out with the help of a trainer what your ideal training zone is. Maybe invest in a heart rate monitor (www.heartratemonitor.co.uk).

Drink!
A lack of water can affect your strength, stamina and ability to burn fat.

Try another idea...

If I can't persuade you to get to the gym, then do it your own way. Check out IDEA 26, *The Hoover work-out*, and IDEA 21, *Out there and doing it*.

Defining idea...

'The worst moment in life is the moment you lose faith in your dreams. Never let it happen.'
MICHAEL COLGAN, specialist in the field of optimum nutrition for US Olympic sports people

Eat!
Don't undo all the good work with a chocolate bar after your work-out. If you're unsure about what to choose see a nutritionist.

Rest!
There is such a thing as overtraining. As you become fitter you may be able to train longer and harder, but muscles need rest to repair, recover and strengthen. Overtraining can deplete the immune system as well as your mood and energy levels.

Ouch!
If you feel pain, especially sustained pain, see someone about it – gym staff are the first port of call. Pain is the body's way of telling you something is wrong, so don't ignore it.

Idea 24 – Geeing up for the gym

Q **My main aim is to get slimmer. Aside from working harder or longer, how can I get the most out of my work-out?**

A If fat loss is your primary goal, aim to exercise in the morning before breakfast. That way you'll be using your body's energy stores.

Q **How can I stop myself getting into a rut?**

A Mix it up. Depending on how often you're going to the gym, vary the body parts you train. So, if you train your upper body one day, train your lower body next time. Don't train the same section for two consecutive days. Maybe you should try interval training, which is an effective and fun way to burn fat and increase stamina. Incorporate short bursts of high-impact cardiovascular work in between your weight training. This may only last two to three minutes, but it's a great way to improve your heart rate variability.

How did it go?

52 Brilliant Ideas – **Get healthy for good**

25
Stretching the point

Stretching is one of those things we know we should do, don't really know why and quietly forget about when no one's looking.

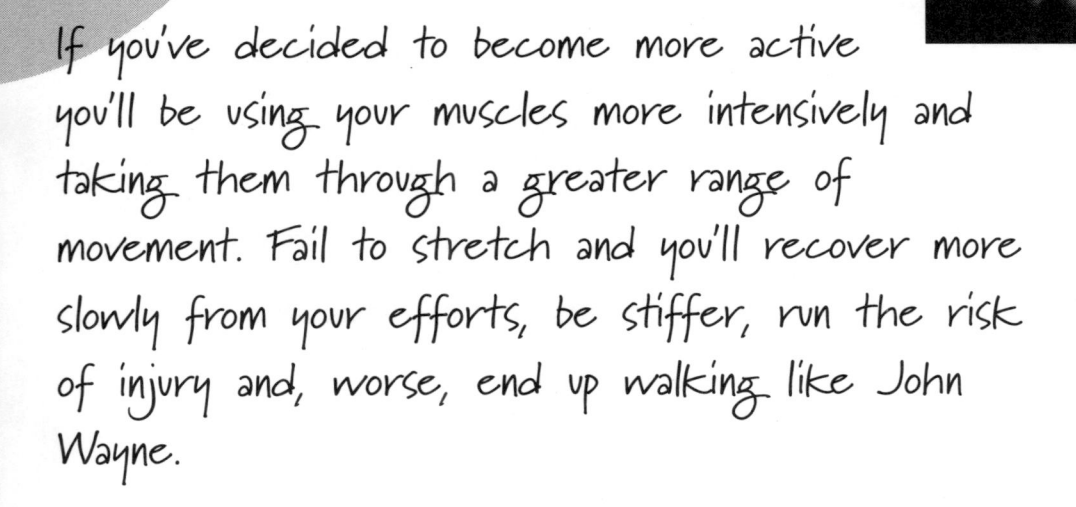

If you've decided to become more active you'll be using your muscles more intensively and taking them through a greater range of movement. Fail to stretch and you'll recover more slowly from your efforts, be stiffer, run the risk of injury and, worse, end up walking like John Wayne.

TYPES OF STRETCHING

Pre-stretches
These prepare your body for what's to come. There's a lot of argument about this since many people, including myself, think you run more risk of damaging yourself by stretching when cold than actually doing any good. Similarly, while many gyms

> **Here's an idea for you...**
> If you like the idea of developmental stretching and would like to be suppler, try Bikram yoga. Sessions are conducted in a steamy room to keep muscle temperatures high and help suppleness. There's only one set of moves so it's easy to learn but takes forever to master. The emphasis is on developing the range of movement and stretch in joints and muscles.

offer a 'stretching' class, very few will make sure you warm up properly beforehand. So, if you're going to do a stretching class then make sure you warm up thoroughly (jog, row, cycle) so that the appropriate areas are really ready to rumble.

Maintenance stretch

This is done at the end of your exercise or during it in the form of stretch breaks (very handy for a sneaky excuse to catch your breath). The aim of maintenance stretching is to help your muscles resume their normal length after working harder. You should hold the stretch for just 10 to 15 seconds or so. Remember to stretch all of the muscles you're using – for example, new runners often remember to stretch their legs, but forget the hip flexors at the top of the pelvis that are used to raise the knee in the direction of the chest.

Developmental stretching

This is all about trying to stretch the muscles further and longer so they become more flexible and better at your chosen activity. Start stretching as normal and hold the stretch for 8–10 seconds while your muscle relaxes into the new position. Then go further into the stretch and continue the count up to 20 seconds to complete the stretch.

Idea 25 – **Stretching the point**

COMMON STRETCHES

There's a stretch for every part of your body, including a few you're probably not familiar with yet. Take time to find out about the stretches specific to your sport and then take the time to do them. The most common stretches are:

Quadriceps
Whilst standing upright, balance on one leg and bend the other so you can catch your foot in your hand. Flex your foot gently back up to your buttocks and don't worry about putting a hand out on a wall or partner to keep your balance. Very slightly bend the knee of the leg you're balancing on and tip the hips forward to feel the stretch down the front of your thigh. Hold. Gently go back to standing and switch legs.

Calves
Stand four or five steps away from and facing a wall. Keep your left foot in its original position but place your right foot halfway between you and the wall. Reach forward with your outstretched arms so you're leaning against the wall with them. Your right leg should now be bent and your left leg straight out behind you with the sole of the foot flat on the floor. Feel the stretch up the back of the calf. Hold, then gently go back to standing and switch legs.

If you're keen to improve your fitness and suppleness look at IDEA 24, *Geeing up for the gym*.

Try another idea...

'When you engage in systematic, purposeful action, using and stretching your abilities to the maximum, you cannot help but feel positive and confident about yourself.'
BRIAN TRACY, US author and motivational speaker

Defining idea...

111

Triceps
Reach one arm straight up above your head then bend it at the elbow so your hand is now behind your neck. Reach up with the other hand, take the first elbow, and gently pull it down and across in the direction of the pulling arm's shoulder. Hold, release, switch.

Shoulder
Hold your arm out straight in front of you then move it across your body placing the other hand on the upper arm between elbow and shoulder. Use that hand to push the arm in towards the chest. Hold, release, switch.

How did it go?

Q **I hurt when I stretch, is this right?**

A *Absolutely not. Never go into a stretch to the point where it hurts. You should feel the stretching, but actual pain is never a good thing. Gently build the stretch up little by little over a matter of weeks until you can get to the point where you stretch that far without hurting.*

Q **At school we used to 'bounce' into stretches to get a bit further than normal. Is this still a good idea?**

A *By and large, no. Professional athletes in explosive sports like jumping and sprinting use so-called 'ballistic' stretches, but for the rest of us it's just an invitation to injury.*

26
The Hoover work-out

Why not make a real difference to your fitness by grabbing all the everyday opportunities?

The gym is great, but it's exercise in a structured, get-all-the-right-kit sort of way.

I actually hate going to the gym. I find myself joining up in winter, then at some point in June finally going for my very expensive swim, having felt guilty about not going for the last six months!

I know it's obvious, but walking is a great way to up the exercise and doesn't demand any special kit or skills. Here's a really good life tip from a London cabby I spoke to last week:

The cabby had a fifteen-stone wife until she decided to go for a walk with her friend three times a week. Each session lasted for an hour. It wasn't a pushing-it-walk mind, but a little bit more than a stroll. She'd piled on the pounds since having her two children and had tried every diet under the sun. So, she decided to give up the diets, eat a wee bit more sensibly and take up walking. Five months later and she is

Here's an idea for you...

Dancing is both a great way to burn off those calories and a great de-stressor, so get out there and strut your stuff. Added bonuses are meeting people and forgetting about any worries for an entire evening!

just under ten stone, without doing anything more complicated than going for a walk down by the river where she lives. She finds that walking is a great de-stressor too and manages to combine it with a gossip with her friend. She also loves the peace and quiet away from the kids, who she dumps on her hubby for an hour, scooting out the door with a cheery wave.

Depending on where you live and work, a great way to carve the time out is to walk to work. As you won't really get sweaty, you won't have to worry about shower facilities as you might following a session down the gym. I carry a clean top in my rucksack and put my wallet, keys and 'handbag' stuff in there too. Put on a good pair of gym shoes, put your smart work ones in the rucksack, and off you go. Since I live in Fulham, which is West London, and have to walk to my clinic, which is in Central London, I allow about an hour and a half for my walk. If I'm going to walk, I usually walk there and then take transport back – I find that the flesh is quite willing in the morning, but by the evening I find all sorts of excuses to wriggle out of it. Taking the bus into Central London takes almost the same amount of time as walking, and taking the Underground is OK if you happen to be a sardine but quite an unpleasant experience otherwise. I find that walking to work is a time for me to digest my thoughts. I actually take a small Dictaphone with me so that if I have any ideas I can get them down for processing later on in the day. I really miss my walk when my schedule throws me off track – I'm quite addicted to it.

Idea 26 - **The Hoover work-out**

STRUT YOUR FUNKY STUFF!

Find everyday excuses for exercise at home too. I put on Meat Loaf's *Bat out of Hell*, get the Hoover out and wiggle my stuff about in that dust. And no doubt you've heard it before but walk the escalators, walk up stairs, don't take the lift. Thin, lithe folk are always in motion – be like them. We're designed to be in continuous movement.

Take walking up a notch and check out IDEA 27, *Take a walk on the wild side*.

Try another idea...

Check out the gym again and consider whether you could get into it this time. Look at IDEA 24, *Geeing up for the gym*.

...and another

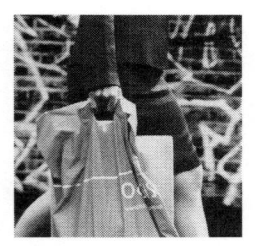

'These are my new shoes. They're good shoes. They won't make you rich like me, they won't make you rebound like me, they definitely won't make you handsome like me. They'll only make you have shoes like me. That's it.'
CHARLES BARKLEY, US basketball player

Defining idea...

115

How did it go?

Q **I'm a new mum and can't spare the time to go to the gym to exercise. In fact, I have no time at all. Any suggestions for the time-poor?**

A Do a baby-and-pram work-out. If you have a dog, get him involved too. In fact, exercise the whole family. Get into some fitness gear so you know it's going to be a work-out rather than simply a walk. Get to your local park if you're in a town or anywhere with flat surfaces that's away from main roads. If you can get hold of a heart rate monitor so much the better as then you'll be able to check that you're actually working out and not just using the time to look at the birds and nature! Aim to run/jog while pushing the pram, working up your times gradually.

Q **Any other suggestions to squeeze in some exercise?**

A What about walking to the shops instead of taking the car? I'm an embarrassment to my friends and family as I take a small wheely suitcase with me to the shops (I haven't quite graduated to the OAP trolley yet!). Remember, even a 15-minute walk is contributing to your total amount of exercise.

27
Take a walk on the wild side

Exercise doesn't have to involve sheathing yourself in Lycra and pounding mindlessly to hip-hop backbeats in front of banks of TV screens.

For centuries, the daily constitutional (walk) was the best way to stay in peak condition whilst at the same time gaining a bit of perspective on life. In many ways it still is.

Walking can mean more than popping out to the corner shop for twenty Marlboro. Why not take a chance on adventure walking? Even if you only plan a walking weekend every so often – a special weekend in the country once or twice a year – it will inspire you for the smaller everyday stuff like getting out to the park or walking to work. You will need to make sure you have your ducks in a row before you start. I'm talking about finding some great countryside and going for it, but making sure you're kitted out with the right gear before you set out. It's unlikely you'll kick off with a life-or-death hike across the Arctic tundra, but wherever you are, you do need to spare a thought for your safety.

> **Here's an idea for you...**
>
> Take a holiday that includes guided walks in wonderful countryside. Lots of companies offer this sort of thing now: try www.atg-oxford.co.uk, which offers walks for all levels of fitness and experience. Also check out www.walkworldwide.com and www.theultimatetravelcompany.co.uk.

EQUIPMENT FOR YOUR OWN MIRACLE

One of the first steps to take (excuse the pun) is to make sure that you have all the right gear. And great wet-weather gear is a must. I'm not talking fisherman's yellow galoshes and capes – these days you can get very light wet-weather gear that will fold up and fit into your pocket. Don't just get the top, invest in the trousers as well – you'll thank me for this one day, as there's nothing worse than being in the middle of nowhere with wet, cold and soggy trousers and no chance of changing them for the next 50 miles. There's no such thing as bad weather, just inappropriate gear!

The second vital bit of kit for your proper walking experience is the right boots. Remember that you could well have thick socks to allow for so don't buy them too small. Talking of socks, it's worth getting proper walking socks. A good outdoor shop should be able to advise you on the right kind of boots and socks for you. The boots need to be protective of the ankles, waterproof and not too heavy. They also need a good grip – the proper lace-up ones are ideal (check out www.snowandrock.com).

Idea 27 - **Take a walk on the wild side**

The other essential piece of kit is your rucksack or daypack. Choose one with a middle strap that goes round your tummy as this will help to protect your back. These days there are rucksacks that make sure that the material isn't next to your back so you don't get too sweaty carrying it. Make sure you get one with loads of pockets for maps, bits of string, etc. Also make sure you have basic survival gear: matches (in a little plastic bag so they're not soggy when you need them), a Swiss army knife, foil blankets, water bottles, oatcakes, nuts and maybe some dark chocolate (temperature permitting). Also, pack a whistle just in case you need to attract attention. And a hat, good sunglasses and some sunscreen. A map is always a good idea, as long as you can read it! And you'll need to carry at least a litre of water. Obviously in boiling temperatures you'll need more. Don't forget to pack a small medical kit that includes some rehydration sachets (electrolyte formulas) and some plasters for those pesky blisters.

IDEA 26, *The Hoover work-out*, will show you how an everyday work-out can help. And IDEA 21, *Out there and doing it*, will reiterate that the gym isn't the only answer.

Try another idea...

'You cannot teach a crab to walk in a straight line.'
ARISTOPHENES

Defining idea...

119

52 Brilliant Ideas – **Get healthy for good**

How did it go?

Q I don't feel brave enough to go it alone on a big walk. How might I find like-minded people?

A Check out your local paper for any conservation groups you could join. You could then go on organised walks with them and at the same time learn a thing or two about the countryside.

Q I don't have the time to go on long walks. Plus all this gear sounds like a fag to organise. How can I get motivated?

A Put actual dates in your diary and organise to go walking with friends. Going on long walks can seem quite scary if you're new to them and can't read a map, but the gear is only necessary if you're going to take the whole thing seriously as obviously short walks in the countryside on designated footpaths don't need full-on survival gear. Always take water with you, however!

120

28
Preposterous posture

Were you always nagged to sit up straight and stop slouching? If you didn't listen, chances are you're now suffering from an even bigger pain in the neck.

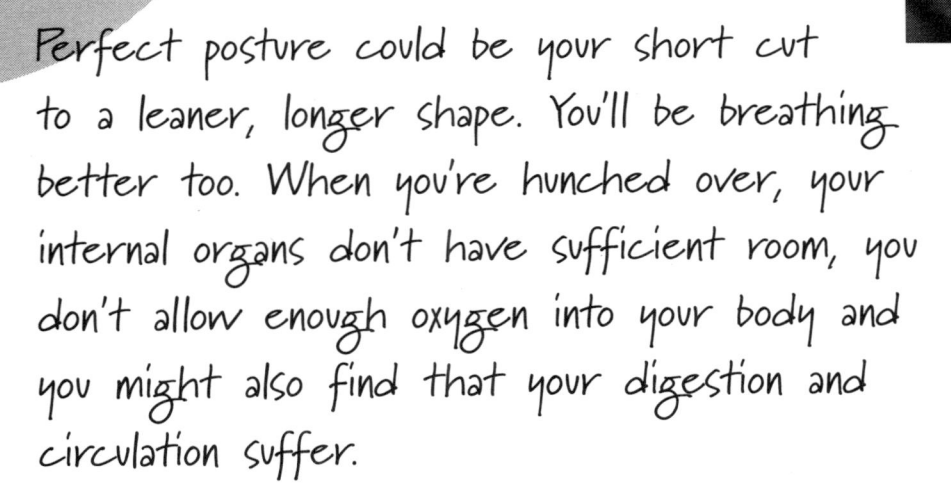

Perfect posture could be your short cut to a leaner, longer shape. You'll be breathing better too. When you're hunched over, your internal organs don't have sufficient room, you don't allow enough oxygen into your body and you might also find that your digestion and circulation suffer.

Try this: Sit up straight for five minutes with your head up and shoulders dropped. Concentrate on your breathing. How do you feel? Relaxed? Of course you do! So, where can you take it next?

Here's an idea for you... **Experiment with different methods of postural improvement by getting DVDs of your new fads. If you enjoy doing a particular discipline in the comfort of your own home take a course of classes where you start right from the beginning and master the basics – it can be very demotivating if everyone is better than you, despite the fact that most posture disciplines profess not to be competitive.**

PILATES

Pilates seems to be the new buzzword, although Joseph H. Pilates actually perfected his programme in the US in the 1920s. Pilates is a re-education programme for your muscles, which are used to a lifetime of abuse. It aims, through often very subtle movements, to correct these bad habits. One of the major features of Pilates is core stability and strength and one of the most difficult things to grasp is the pelvic tilt. In my opinion, you really need a teacher to take you through the basics of Pilates or you can end up wondering whether you're getting it right. Most gyms offer Pilates – take advantage of their classes because one-to-one Pilates tuition can be expensive.

ALEXANDER TECHNIQUE

Think how easily small kids move. However, as we grow older and tense ourselves up against the worries of the world our posture suffers, often with disastrous results such as migraine, arthritis, neck pain and back pain. Many postural problems have stemmed from over-tensed neck muscles, which interfere with how the head relates to the spine. The Alexander Technique is often taught using verbal instruction and the physical guidance of a teacher's correcting hands. It's often taught privately so prepare yourself for an investment. Check out www.alexandertechnique.com, a comprehensive source of information.

JUST BE WITH T'AI CHI

T'ai chi is a slow-moving choreography and is considered a martial art – each minute movement shifts the body's weight subtly from one leg to the other throughout the whole routine. Moment to moment attention is required at all times, thus t'ai chi is a type of meditation through movement. Practised properly, flexibility, balance and strength are all within your grasp. Think of the hundreds practising in groups in China, all silently moving in harmony – wonderful. Look for t'ai chi advertised locally. Again, many gyms now run classes. Be warned, t'ai chi is a lifelong journey, not something you master overnight.

DON'T WANT TO DO THE WORK?

What about getting a chiropractor, osteopath or physiotherapist to check your posture out and help fix it? Over time the lines between these three disciplines seem to have become a little blurred, but a chiropractor is really concerned about your spine; osteopathic treatment concentrates on the relationship between the structure of the body – the skeleton, muscles, ligaments and connective tissues – and relieving muscle tension is often a big part of the therapy; and physiotherapists can assess your posture but often make you do the work itself by giving you exercises to do at home, so this isn't so much for the lazy or undisciplined!

> Let's not forget yoga – check out IDEA 32, *Yoga*.

Try another idea...

> '*Never grow a wishbone, daughter, where your backbone ought to be.*'
> CLEMENTINE PADDLEFORD, author

Defining idea...

How did it go?

Q **I can't decide what posture-busting method I should go for. Any ideas on how to choose?**

A You simply have to suck it and see, but do consider the nature of what you want to do and the type of person you are. Remember that you'll often have to do these disciplines over a long period so choose something you like. If you have no patience then a dynamic form of yoga might suit you, but if you have the patience of a saint then t'ai chi might be your bag.

Q **I train at the gym so don't have time for these types of stretching exercises. And on the rare occasion that I have found the time, I haven't really felt like I've had a proper work-out. Am I doing something wrong?**

A In my opinion you can't afford to pump it down the gym without doing these types of stretching exercises. I call it the ying and yang of exercise – you have to get the balance. Go ahead and do a pumping, thumping work-out, but feed in at least one proper posture session once a week. So, if you do three gym sessions a week, make that two plus an exercise session aimed at looking after your posture.

29
Delegate your way to wellbeing

It's tempting to try and do everything perfectly. Unless you're superhuman, however, this could lead to one very tense life.

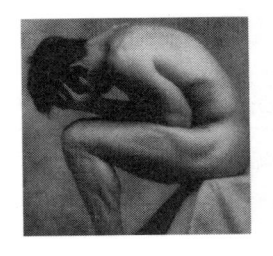

Instead, I suggest you recognise your limitations. Do some things well, some things perfectly and some things really, really badly. Admit to yourself that you need help sometimes and delegate responsibilities or tasks to someone who can do them better.

Often time really is money so if you're working in full time and earning good money and also doing all the cleaning and washing at weekends, ask yourself why. Isn't your time better spent recuperating ready for the week ahead? Isn't it time that you got someone in to help you with the cleaning, ironing and housework?

> **Here's an idea for you...**
>
> If you don't have the patience to wade through self-help books, delegate your self-help to tapes. Try Innertalk (www.innertalk.com), a great company with hundreds of titles to choose from. It uses technology to enhance the messages your subconscious mind is taking on board.

The best way to find a cleaner is still word of mouth, but putting a card up in your local newsagent is a good idea, as long as you follow up references. You don't want just any old bod coming into your house! Once you have a cleaner, you might find you have more time to go to the gym. Schedule gym appointments in the diary – spending the extra time in bed may be great once in a while, but if you do this every weekend, you'll not be making the best of your time. Remember, you're the most important person in your life, so keep appointments you make for yourself.

Get ahead by knowing what you can and can't achieve in a day. No one is judging you – you don't have to be the perfect wife and have the perfect home, kids and full-time job. The Perfect Police aren't just about to raid your premises. Once you realise that life will go on whether or not the sitting room is vacuumed, your life will become a whole lot less stressful.

FOOD GLORIOUS FOOD!

Trying to adopt a new eating regime is difficult to do by yourself. It often takes a lot of change to turn around your eating habits, so why not enlist the help of a nutritionist to guide you through the mire? Two great books to get you started are Patrick Holford's *Optimum Nutrition Bible* and Andrew Weil's *Eight Weeks to Optimum Health*. Both have good resource sections.

Idea 29 – **Delegate your way to wellbeing**

I know you'll want to do it all perfectly, but remember sometimes you can't. That goes for both food preparation and shopping. Shopping online for food makes life easier and saves you valuable time too. And you can make convenience foods more nutritious by adding your own healthy ingredients. For example, you can spice up fresh soups (bought) by adding your own vegetable mix. I even know someone who adds a tin of tuna to her soup bowl to make the soup more filling. Each to their own!

Looking to chill out a little more? Take a look at IDEA 32, Yoga.

Try another idea...

THE PERSONAL POWER OF A TRAINER

If you can't motivate yourself to stay on track in the gym, consider a personal trainer. Even once a week will help make sure you stay on track. Although personal training is expensive, think about how much money you'll waste if you don't use the gym due to a lack of motivation.

THE BATHTUB

Make your bathtime a time where for an hour or so the time and space belong to you. If you can rig up a stereo system into the bathroom and play relaxing music, do it. Don't go without candles and deliciously smelly bath treats!

> *Rest isn't quitting*
> *The busy career,*
> *Rest is the fitting*
> *Of self to one's sphere.*
> JOHN SULLIVAN DWIGHT, nineteenth-century musician

Defining idea...

How did it go?

Q **I don't really have the money to delegate my tasks out to other people. What do you suggest instead?**

A   Without wanting to state the obvious, get your partner or family on side. I've seen some mothers trying to do everything themselves – job, cooking, bedtime, bathtime – whilst cursing the husband and children under their breath, yet not actually asking for any help. Ask, as most people haven't sussed out telepathy yet. I've seen families with rotas drawn up for tasks, with everyone expected to pull their weight, but remember to start early with kids on this one otherwise it'll be impossible to drag them away from the TV without a revolution on your hands.

Q **I think I'm a control freak. I feel if I delegate then things might not be done the way I like them. How can I get round this?**

A   Look at your stress levels. A qualified nutritionist could arrange for you to do an adrenal stress profile, which is a non-invasive test that uses saliva to check your stress hormones. Alternatively, go directly to Individual Wellbeing Diagnostic Laboratories (www.iwdl.net). Incorporating some stress-busting techniques into your life could be helpful, such as relaxation, exercise and healthy eating. Remember that all life's troubles and grief come from attaching to the past too strongly, so start to let go and develop a sense of trust.

Idea 29 – **Delegate your way to wellbeing**

129

52 Brilliant Ideas – **Get healthy for good**

30
Human racing

Today many races are about comradeship, motivation, fun (yes, really) and perhaps the chance to do something for charity. Oh, and you get to bask in glory and show off your prize.

There are people who swim, cycle or run all their lives yet never race and then there are those for whom no weekend seems complete without one. It takes all types. However, those who do try a race will usually do more. And here's why.

Races these days really are about the taking part more than the winning. Sure there will be enviably fast uber-athletes fighting it out at the front for podium places, but they'll be out of sight so why worry about them? With the right attitude, a race is all about a little excitement, a break from the routine and the chance to run, swim, cycle, rollerblade or whatever with a horde of other people much like yourself. There's a very primitive pleasure in being part of a unified horde trundling towards a goal, and a very strong sense of satisfaction in completing a set goal. Plus, in many cases there's a medal/mug/sweatshirt to take out and cherish when no one's looking.

Here's an idea for you...

Other racing options include 'super-sprint' triathlons, which are open to anyone who can swim, cycle and run or walk. Take a look online for your national triathlon organisation and chances are you'll find a calendar of events and details of each discipline. There are also duathlon events for non-swimmers and a few aquathlon events for the bicycle-intolerant.

Finding a race is easy. Most running magazines contain calendars of forthcoming races and if you can't get hold of one of these, then there are loads of websites that can help you (try www.coolrunning.com). Choosing a race is a different matter. The distance is likely to be your primary consideration but don't forget things like the flatness (or otherwise) of the course. Be very wary of any course described as 'undulating' – one man's undulation is another man's mountain. Think carefully before travelling to a race. When will you get there? Will you be rested before your race? Even old hands get nervous before a race and it can take just a small thing to tip the balance over into stress, which isn't the idea at all. Here are a few pointers to make life easier for your first race:

- Find a friend of similar ability to do the race with. This'll give you a shared pleasure and reduce stress enormously.

- Enlist a friend who isn't racing to cheer you on, find you at the end and act as a mobile locker room.

- Find out where the toilets are before the race. This might sound funny, but you will need to go and the last thing you want is to be rushing around trying to find them. And take a wad of toilet paper in case the local facilities have run out (as usual).

Idea 30 - **Human racing**

- Take some safety pins so you can pin your number on your top.

- Take a snack bar to munch on an hour before you race and another one to polish off when you've finished the race.

- Don't go out and get larruped the night before through nerves or excitement

- Have a good meal the night before and try to sleep well.

- Don't wear any new items of clothing, especially shoes. Race day is the time for tried and trusted.

- Don't go off too fast.

- Don't forget to stretch at the end (easily forgotten in all the excitement), as you don't want the satisfaction of your race to be dimmed by walking like John Wayne for the following week.

- Above all, take the time to enjoy the whole thing. As you go round, remember to think to yourself, 'This is me doing this, me.' Make sure you have a celebration planned for afterwards. It doesn't matter how you do, just the fact that you did it makes you a winner and you deserve to bask in your own glory.

Try another idea...

If you're going to run a race you should be aware of the importance of stretching – see IDEA 25, Stretching the point.

Defining idea...

'Plodding wins the race.'
AESOP

133

How did it go?

Q **I'm afraid of coming last. What can I do about it?**

A Worry less about the physical side of the race and concentrate more on your mindset. Look to your own performance and let the others worry about theirs. As the old adage says: it's the taking part that counts, not the winning.

Q **I'm fine about the race itself but our local dash starts at the local school. I haven't been in a communal shower since I left school, let alone queued for one. The thought puts me right off, is there any other way?**

A Certainly. Lots of runners and racers don't worry about grabbing a shower at the end, they just throw on a clean T-shirt, cover up with a track suit and wait until they get home. The smart ones also take along a tub of wet wipes.

31

Get on yer bike

It's difficult to injure yourself cycling because it's such a low-impact form of exercise, plus it's a great way to tone your legs and the nicest way to see the countryside.

Cycling will also strengthen your heart, lower your blood pressure, boost your energy, burn off extra fat and reduce stress. So, what are you waiting for? Get on yer bike!

STRETCH IT OUT

Some cyclists, particularly those of you who hop on your bikes and cycle to work, rarely bother to warm up. If this is you, you might want to take a long hard look at your flexibility and posture. The main thigh muscle (the rectus femoris) has a high chance of being damaged unless you stretch it out properly. Another thing to watch out for is tight hamstrings and pulled hip flexors (at the top of the front of the thigh), which can happen often if you don't take time to stretch. A heel dig stretch might help as a basic exercise to help all three of these common muscle problems.

Here's an idea for you...

If cycling gets your wheels turning consider combining it with a holiday. Find a company that'll give you an itinerary suited to your energy level plus accompanying cars to drop off your baggage at the next hotel on the route, then all you'll have to do is pedal and enjoy the view.

Simply lift your toes, keeping your knee straight and your heel on the ground, until you feel a pull in the back and front of the calf and upper thigh.

Hunching at the handlebars can lead to a permanent rounding of the shoulders and back. A typical yoga exercise can help counter act this – the Cobra. Lie on your front with your arms by your sides and lift your chest and head until you feel the movement in your back and shoulders. Don't forget to cool down properly too. Don't come to an abrupt halt, since your blood will pool in your legs. Instead, slow down gradually and finish with a few minutes of the heel dig stretch.

Idea 31 – **Get on yer bike**

GETTING THE RIGHT BIKE FOR YOU

Your choice of bike depends on what you want your bike for. Mountain bikes are rarely suitable for riding in town and that goes for racing bikes too, however flash they may look. Having your head down when you ride is a sure way of going headlong into a bus! If you've splashed out on a new bike, consider getting it sprayed with nasty black paint in order to stop other people thinking what a beautiful new bike you have and stealing it.

Swallow saddles (www.brooksengland.com) are back in vogue. These are long pointy saddles with an unfeasibly small sitting area that must owe more to aesthetics than to comfort as I imagine it's akin to sitting on a knife. I recommend looking at a seat that has a three-layered saddle of gel/foam/elastic that reduces pressure on the prostate and pubic bones (www.lookin.it). Aaah, that's more like it!

Try another idea...

If you want cycling to make a difference to your fitness, consider getting a heart rate monitor. See IDEA 22, **Have a heart (rate monitor).**

Defining idea...

'There's no such thing as bad weather – only bad wet weather gear.'
A piece of traditional outdoor wisdom

137

How did it go?

Q **I'd love to cycle, but I'm terrified of being squashed by a car. How can I feel safer?**

A Getting the right gear is paramount to making you feel safe. Wearing a helmet is vital – most accidents on bikes resulting in serious injury involve unnecessary head injuries. Also get yourself a bright fluorescent jacket or a reflective strip. Back and front lights are the law, but make sure they're good ones – it's all about being seen. Don't ride along hugging the curb, as this will encourage cars to ignore you. Within reason, own your lane so that cars have to make a conscious effort to pull out and pass you properly, like they would another car, giving you plenty of space. When you're passing parked cars, keep a particular eye out for people suddenly opening their car doors, another good reason for allowing plenty of room around you when you ride.

Q **I often consider cycling, but wet weather puts me off. Do you have any wet-weather solutions?**

A Get some good lightweight waterproofs. Nowadays you don't have to look like an angler expecting a force 12 gale as waterproofs are made of extremely lightweight material, which folds up into a very small bundle. (Peake do good gear.) Get both top and bottoms and even consider waterproof shoe covers. Clear goggles are also a good idea, as they'll stop water or stones being flicked up into your eyes. You might not look beautiful with all this gear on, but you'll certainly be dry!

32

Yoga

Yoga is about being rather than doing. It's non-competitive and a great balancer for the type of exercise you might do at the gym.

Not so long ago, if you admitted you did yoga you'd have been classed as a New Age weirdo and given a wide berth. Today, if you're not into yoga you're the weird one. So, get with the programme!

Although Yoga has evolved to incorporate quite a few different types, you're missing the point if you're using yoga to 'get a work-out'. Check out www.yogapoint.com for a guide to all the different types of yoga and pick the one that sounds interesting for you. You might want to experiment with the different types by going to a few classes. Or ask around, as friends might be able to give you advice.

In essence though, all types of yoga are about using the body and breathing to help calm the mind in order to produce a feeling of wellbeing. Yoga is a great stress buster if ever there was one and it's easy to do at any age so it's never too late to start. Flexibility is a vital component, both physically and mentally – a flexible mind equals a flexible body. Yoga generally uses asanas (postures) that usually retain their ancient names: the fish, the bridge, the bow, the scorpion, etc. They are believed to bring benefits to different areas of the body and are held for a period of time to stretch and strengthen muscles. The shoulder-stand asana, for example, is said to massage the thyroid and bring benefits to the mind through improving blood circulation to the head. Worth a try? The simplest asana is the corpse position, which involves lying down on your back on the floor with your eyes closed. Your breathing should be slow and steady, and your arms should be held at a 45-degree angle away from the body.

Here's an idea for you... As an alternative to hiring a private teacher, which can be quite expensive, club together with a couple of friends for some really worthwhile tuition in a small group once a week. You can always go to classes at the gym the rest of the time.

...and another If you're disciplined and motivated use tapes and DVDs at home. It obviously depends on the type of yoga you settle on, but Sivananda centres offer good tapes.

Idea 32 – **Yoga**

Yoga is really a lifestyle rather than simply an exercise discipline. It incorporates 'proper' breathing or relaxation and a 'proper' diet. It's powerful stuff that's deceptively simple and amazingly dynamic. A proper diet, according to the yogis, is usually a vegetarian diet comprising Sattic foods such as wholemeal grains and fresh fruit and vegetables. Diet as a whole is divided up into three main sections: Sattic foods, which I've already mentioned; Rajasic foods, which are hot and bitter foods (e.g. coffee, tea, chocolate, salt, strong herbs, fish) that are considered to destroy the mind–body equilibrium; and Tamasic foods (e.g. meat, alcohol, garlic, onions), which neither benefit the mind nor the body as they encourage a sense of inertia. Stale or unripe food is also considered Tamasic.

Why not look at IDEA 28, Preposterous posture, on yoga's younger cousin Pilates. And if you're interested in the breathing side of things, see IDEA 48, Breathe in, breathe out!

Try another idea...

'Asanas make one firm, free from maladies, light of limb.'
HATHA YOGA PRDIPIKA

Defining idea...

'The soul that moves in the world of senses in harmony...finds rest in quietness.'
BHAGAVAD GITA

Defining idea...

141

How did it go?

Q **I'd really like to take yoga further. What do you suggest?**

A Why not go on a yoga holiday? There's a lot of them about, but I like The Hill That Breathes (www.thehillthatbreathes.com), which combines yoga with great food and wine in the beautiful Italian countryside. Otherwise, good books that I like include The Book of Yoga – The Complete Step-by-Step Guide by The Sivananda Centre, which has loads of pictures.

Q **I'm pregnant. Can I still do yoga?**

A Yes, but do ask a qualified yoga teacher which exercises are suitable and which ones you should avoid, as it's really important not to strain yourself. There are often special pregnancy classes and I'd suggest you check out Sivananda (www.sivananda.org), which has a centre in most countries and many major cities.

33
Games other people play

If you left sports and team games behind with teenage crushes, acne and underage drinking, then perhaps you're missing out.

I hated games at school and still have nightmares about muddy fields, skinned knees and sadistic gym teachers. Above all I could have been doing other more pleasurable things instead like watching telly and dreaming about the opposite sex.

There was a problem with the way sports were taught at my school. Those that were any good at it were groomed and encouraged, possibly to the point where they became heartily sick of sport. Those who weren't so good were sidelined because the emphasis was always firmly on winning – winning against other kids and winning against other schools. Something tells me my school's approach wasn't so unusual. As an adult, however, you have the option of taking up a sport simply for the pleasure of it. If you take up a new game now, you don't have to be good at it, you simply have to enjoy it. You'll find a club at your level for most adult team

Here's an idea for you...

Think hard about what sports you might enjoy – there's a lot more to sport than football or tennis. Why not try your hand at something really different? If you enjoyed messing around in the pool but were never very good at swimming, consider Octopush – underwater hockey. No matter how good someone is, their time 'on the ball' will end when they run out of breath and have to resurface.

...and another

Consider the likes of roller hockey, fencing and Gaelic games, as sports that are completely different from anything you did when younger won't come with any historical baggage, including preconceived ideas about whether or not it matters to be good at it.

games, and it's likely to be one that will be profoundly grateful that you show up at all. In return, you'll get a chance to break out of your old routine and be more active. Sports aren't just about fitness either. For many, sport is a means of making new friends or getting away from their normal lives. Some even use sport as a means of travel – I know at least one football team that exists mainly to go on 'tours' where they play against similarly minded teams (usually those formed in pubs and bars) abroad.

RACQUET GAMES

For many of us the idea of playing a sport leads directly to thoughts of tennis or squash, which is great except that almost all racquet games are sprint sports that require skill, stamina and explosive strength. They can be great fun and they have a social world all of their own, but to get the most out of them you really need to get fit to play them, rather than play them to get fit. Unless you have a solid background in these sports, you may want to start off with a coach to pick up the rules and techniques. Also, have you ever considered badminton? Although it can be a very fast game, it's about the only racquet game that can truly be played leisurely between like-minded people. Why not try it, even if only to use it as a warm-up to something more energetic?

If you want to get active but prefer to do it on your own, take a look at IDEA 23, *Gotta run*.

Try another idea...

BALL GAMES

Ball games like football (soccer) or rugby are also sprint sports where walking and jogging alternate with sprinting. Instead of going straight for the main game, you may find there's more knockabout fun to be had from smaller versions of the sport like five-a-side footie or seven-a-side rugby. There are also less-aggressive versions, such as 'touch' rugby, plus long-standing gender gaps are finally breaking down with women's football and rugby teams thriving worldwide.

BOWLING

Bowling isn't the world's most active activity, but it's social, gets you active, and can be applied to different games depending on where you are. Lawn bowling has a more sedate image, though the skills aren't dissimilar from its more youthful ten-pin cousin, and the French game of boules can now be seen on beaches and in local clubs around the planet. The great thing about something like ten-pin bowling is that anyone can have a go and the kit you need (bowls and bowling shoes) will be provided by the bowling hall.

'Any kind of exercise is generally better than no exercise at all. Walking is better for you than sitting in front of a television set and playing a sport is better for your health than just being a spectator.'
ARNOLD SCHWARZENEGGER

Defining idea...

How did it go?

Q **I quite fancy the idea of taking up a new sport, but I'm worried about making a fool of myself? Won't others laugh at my lack of fitness or skill?**

A   If you find a club that laughs at newcomers then find another one that isn't so pleased with itself. There are clubs aimed at every level of fitness and skill so go along to a club and watch, taking the time to talk to the club secretary about who plays. Chances are they'll do all they can to encourage you, and if they find they have enquiries from a number of 'keen but clueless' people then they'll more than likely try to arrange something for you. If you're really keen you could ask them to refer any other wannabees to you and you could then arrange your own club.

Q **What about the cost of equipment?**

A   Research a club before you spend a penny on a new sport. Find out what kit they can lend you while you find your feet and look for any small ads and word-of-mouth deals for second-hand kit at a fraction of shop prices.

34

Home spa

Why splash out on beauty treatments when you can achieve practically the same result in the comfort of your own home? Create your very own spa, take the phone off the hook, then lie back and enjoy.

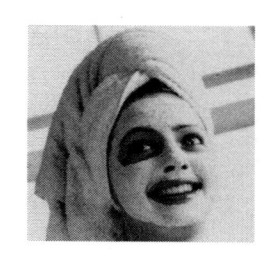

Pick a weekend, invite some girlfriends over and get some healthy food in. This doesn't preclude the guys, however. By all means join us.

WAKE UP YOU LEMON!

First things first, hop out of bed and go and make yourself a cup of hot water with lemon or lime. This will help to eliminate toxins that your body has been busy clearing during the night. You might also decide that a smoothy is in order for a delicious, vitalising breakfast.

Before your bathing rituals, start your morning with a skin-brushing session. As well as keeping the inside in, the skin is an important organ of elimination. Dry skin brushing is a great but inexpensive way to boost blood and lymphatic circulation and remove dead skin cells. Lymphatic fluid brings nutrients to cells and carries

Here's an idea for you... Hang a muslin bag or old sock (a clean one please) filled with porridge oats under the hot tap whilst running your bath. Oats contain properties that are very soothing and moisturising to the skin, especially for those who suffer with dry skin conditions such as eczema. Don't let the porridge fall into the water, as this would be very messy.

away toxins, but isn't pumped by the heart, instead it is moved primarily by movement and massage. The skin may feel a little tender at first, but by jove it's worth it because when you have your cold shower, your skin will tingle all over. Actually, you might want to start with a tepid shower, I won't call you a coward. Remember, you have to suffer to be beautiful and this is helping with the cellulite – so get on with it! Choose a natural bristle brush with a long handle, start at the feet and brush upwards towards the heart in long sweeping figure-of-eight movements. For your arm and chest you are brushing down towards the heart – don't brush any really sensitive bits!

Smell is very important and aromatherapy oils can either be added to yet another bathing experience or added to a little water in a special oil burner and heated gently by a nightlight candle. Be careful though as essential oils are highly flammable. You can get your oils from www.tisserand.com.

Idea 34 – **Home spa**

Treat yourself to a detox clay wrap. Shape Changers (www.shapechangers.co.uk) are a favourite and contain 100% clay with a range of aromatherapy oils. They're designed to cleanse and tone the skin and draw out toxins – check out the inch-loss potential on this one!

IDEA 13, *Ready for a detox?*, is an absolute must-read as it would be great to do a detox alongside your home spa. IDEA 10, *Skin from within*, is also worth a squint.

Try another idea...

In the afternoon go to your local gym for a sauna or a steam and, if you're not sick of the whole detox experience, before you go to bed strap on two detox plasters (www.koyotakara.com) to the soles of your feet. When you wake the next morning, you'll be horrified to find brown gunky stuff on the plaster, which is your own personal toxin dump.

'Beauty is only skin deep.'
A traditional saying, but who cares?

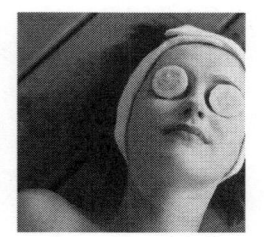

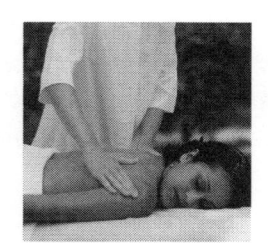

Defining idea...

149

How did it go?

Q **Beauty products tend to be expensive. Is there something I can use for my home spa that won't cost a fortune?**

A Epsom salts (magnesium sulphate) when added to the bath draws toxins from the body, relaxes muscles and is a natural sedative for the body. You need to add about a kilo of salts to your bath water and soak for half an hour. The best time to have an Epsom Salts bath is just before bed to promote relaxation and deep sleep.

Q **I've heard about the benefits of exfoliating. How can I do this effectively?**

A Salt scrubs are great for this, but choose one that doesn't include mineral oil but has an alternative base such as jojoba or sunflower oil. Don't go for the ones with a very heavy fragrance either.

Q **How can I make the skin on my face soft?**

A Add water from flower petals to the water you wash your face with – choose rose, camomile or elderflower. The loose varieties that are sold as tea are a good choice. Cucumber and rose facial sprays are great for reviving the face first thing in the morning, just before or after moisturiser, and after a face mask or a steam. They're also fine enough to use on the plane to hydrate your skin and the air around you. They're especially nice when kept in the fridge and used on a hot summer's day.

35

Kool kids kicking

How to get couch potatoes up off the couch and eating their greens.

We've seen it on TV and read it in the newspapers — kids are getting fatter, it's official.

Over the last ten years, the proportion of overweight children in Britain aged under four increased from one sixth to one quarter. So, what's been happening? Well, the Janet and John picture of an idyllic childhood probably went out the window at just about the moment that computer games and TV took over as chief entertainers. First, parents don't have the time. Second, children don't have the time, as schools have become increasingly competitive and exams set for younger and younger age groups.

Schools nowadays generally put less emphasis on sport and some schools have even been seduced by the big fizzy-drinks manufacturers into using school as a battleground for 'brand awareness', fighting for loyalty in vending machines sited in school corridors. No wonder our kids are supersizing along with their extra portions of chips.

Here's an idea for you...

Get your kids into food early and make food fun. Get them to help you prepare food in the kitchen, make up food quizzes or use storytime to talk about food and throw in lines such as, 'Rabbits eat nutritious carrots and you've never seen a rabbit wearing glasses, now have you?' The pull from TV and peer pressure is so great that you must exert your influence or get lost in a sea of chicken nuggets and burgers! Introduce your kids early to non-sweet and non-salty food and they'll actually turn their hooters up at junk food.

HARD WORK?

If you suspect your child is overweight (check out www.keepkidshealthy.com to see if your fears are justified), you might just want to take the 'mote' out of your own eye and get your own house in order. Look at your own eating and exercise habits as children generally take their parents' lead. Perhaps it's time to take a good hard look at the family's lifestyle and do something drastic. Limit TV to a maximum of an hour on school nights and an hour and a quarter at weekends. Use the weekend to get into exercising as a family. Activities such as walking and swimming are easy and fun or joining a running club or a martial arts club (fantastic for kids' confidence). You could even get other parents involved and get a rota going. Taking kids to a farmer's market can be a fun activity and the different sights and colours and will show them 'real' food in a stimulating environment

Never put a young child on a diet as this will often give you and your child problems later on, as they might develop complexes that degenerate into disordered eating. Instead, guide them gently towards healthy choices so that instead of saying 'no' all the time, you're saying 'yes' because of the abundance of fresh fruit and veg available. Preparing vegetables with dips like hummous is a great

Idea 35 – **Kool kids kicking**

way to make kids eat vegetables and making desserts that include fruit is a great way to try and get more portions eaten – apple crumble is easy to make. Make a wall chart listing the colours and number of portions of fruit they've eaten in a week and score it with glittery stars. Consider a non-food treat for plenty of stars at the end of the month.

Although you can't control what happens outside the home, you can control what food your kid comes into contact with inside the home. Therefore, don't keep unhealthy, fattening food at home. Better choices if they seem to need a snack are chopped apple and a small piece of cheese, oatcakes or carrots with hummous, bananas and nuts (nuts aren't suitable for small children as they can choke). Add extra toppings on takeaway pizza to make it more nutritious and more filling, and limit the portion size.

Introducing all of the above early on will save a great deal of pain down the road.

Be inventive with exercise and children. See IDEA 26, *The Hoover work-out*, in this respect. Get them to help you with the housework, but start early or the TV will be the strongest master. Also check out IDEA 20, *Nutrition: the basics*.

Try another idea...

'Give me the child until he is seven, and I will show you the man.'
Jesuit doctrine

Defining idea...

153

How did it go?

Q **Look, I'm a really busy person. How do I have the time to prepare healthy food for my kids?**

A   *If you don't have the time to be in the kitchen baking all day and convenience food is your only choice, start making better choices. For example, choose sausages that are 85% meat and choose low-salt, low-sugar baked beans. Also, choose fillet fish fingers and when a takeaway is called for remove most of the batter and add a vegetable to increase the nutritional value of the meal. With curries, choose plain rice and not fried rice and include a vegetable option for variety.*

Q **I feel that I'm fighting a losing battle with the advertisers influencing what my child will eat. How can I beat the ads?**

A   *Make the advertising work for you and use the same language as the ad man. Cook up your own 'noodle-tastic' treats and make food 'bonkers' too. Make your own chicken nuggets and you too can do noodles in oodles of wonderful tomato sauce. A great book for recipe ideas is* What Should I Feed My Baby? *by Susannah Olivier. Check it out and let the fun begin!*

36

Let's face facts

Skin is your body's biggest organ. It mirrors your inner health and, unlike your other organs, the world gets to look at it.

Pale, blotchy skin says you're not looking after yourself in some respect. You can do much to improve it though from both the outside and inside. It's simply a question of finding the right products for you, then actually using them!

BEFORE WE START

Sunshine – don't we just love it? There are some real health benefits to be had from being in sunshine, but like everything you can have too much of a good thing. The trouble is, sunshine is dehydrating, as hot sun will increase the evaporation of water from the surface of the skin. You need plenty of antioxidants or agents that protect us against harmful environmental factors. These can be found in, you guessed it, fruit and vegetables. Obviously, plenty of water is the order of the day too – at least

Here's an idea for you...

Treat yourself to a facial massage. They're wonderful for the circulation – the Aveda salons (www.aveda.com) are great for this and although they tend to be hellishly expensive, they're well worth the investment in my opinion. Alternatively do it yourself with a home massage – Neal's Yard (www.nealsyardremedies.com) do some great oils, especially the rose face oils. A number of websites give advice on this: Google 'facial massage' and enjoy.

2 litres (3.5 pints) of the stuff. And knock off the cigarettes and the alcohol! You know it is bad for you and it's really not helping your body's detoxification pathways (your liver in particular). One last nag, remember to incorporate lots of essential fatty acids in your diet as your skin needs to be well oiled, so include lots of nuts, seeds and oily fish in your diet.

ROUTINE, ROUTINE!

I remember friends laughing at me at university for using expensive products on my skin. There's nothing wrong with soap and water they cried. The decades take a poor view of soap and water, in my opinion. I've always used expensive products, right from when my mum set me up with my first skincare regime when I was about thirteen. Of course, you don't have to spend a fortune on skincare, and expensive doesn't always equal good, but getting into a routine is vital. I found that my expensive products made me want to use them and their value was reflected in my skin.

Idea 36 – Let's face facts

The second thing I learned very early on in my life was to always take your make-up off, however late you get to bed! When I was fifteen, my best friend Helena stayed over after a party. At four in the morning, there she was carefully taking off all her make-up. She had beautiful clear skin whereas I, already in bed with a smudged party face, had a face like a pizza. From that moment on, regardless of the time, I've always properly cleansed my face.

Look at IDEA 10, *Skin from within*, for the low-down on skin from a diet point of view. IDEA 13, *Ready for a detox?*, might clear out a few cobwebs and find out why you need water in IDEA 11, *Water babies*.

Try another idea...

The most important thing you can do to perk your skin up is to exfoliate. Exfoliation isn't something you need to do every day – once a week should be fine. As we get older, we really need to make sure we're exfoliating on a really regular basis otherwise if we don't clear out the dead cells, wrinkles can look deeper. Older skin too needs a gentler touch when it comes to exfoliation – no pulling and rubbing or harsh products like creams based on fruit acids. Fresh (www.fresh.com) have a really wonderful facial scrub that is moisturising at the same time. Alternatively, make your own exfoliator with 2 teaspoons of fine oatmeal and 2 teaspoons of ground almonds with some rose water to blend. Rub it in small circular motions over your skin, then rinse off.

'You can have anything you want – if you want it badly enough. You can be anything you want to be, do anything you set out to accomplish, if you hold to that desire with singleness of purpose.'
WILLIAM ADAMS (so if you want beautiful skin, start looking after it!)

Defining idea...

How did it go?

Q **My skin really looks dull. What can I do for an instant pick-me-up?**

A Treat yourself to a mask. There are some brilliant ones on the market, but the ones that I love at the moment are REN's Multi-Mineral Detox Facial Mask and REN's Jirgolulan Cell Energising Facial Mask (both available from www.beautyexpert.co.uk).

Q **I've tried everything and my skin still looks dull and flat. Any suggestions?**

A It might be worth investing in a facial. I really like the Clarins' facials as they're usually not the most expensive one yet you still come out with skin that looks like its been on holiday. The extra boost you get from professional help can often prompt you to look after your skin more carefully yourself.

Q **With all this talk about my face, what about my body?**

A A cheap way to exfoliate your skin is to use sea salt as a scrub. Scrub your body all over (avoiding the really sensitive areas) and rinse, if you can stand it, in cold water to give your skin a real tingle.

Idea 36 – **Let's face facts**

52 Brilliant Ideas – **Get healthy for good**

160

37
Dressing for success

What has dressing for success got to do with your whole health? Well, when you're confident and glowing this is a reflection of your state of health and mind.

Poorly turned out says, 'I don't value who I am.' Confident dressing says, 'I've arrived and am ready to grasp life and opportunities to the full!'

You might think that your skimpy belly-baring top is going to win you that top job and set you on your personal road to riches, but remember that, with the exception of top models, most people look truly terrible in anything that exposes their love handles to full effect. In the majority of cases, love handles should be viewed strictly by appointment only.

Dressing for success is mostly about being wonderfully stylish, without looking boring or frumpy. You can still express your personality, but you also need to take in the sensibilities of who is looking at you. Think of yourself as your own personal marketing manager, with you as the product. I'm sure your mum will have nagged you about many of the ground rules: 'Clean face, clean hands and don't forget to brush your hair!'

Here's an idea for you... Get help! Most department stores have personal shoppers who will take you around the store for free. Don't feel embarrassed if your budget is small or if you're only interested in one or two items to build outfits around. That's what they're there for.

GOOD TAILORING

Good tailoring is everything, even if you have only a couple of good things in your wardrobe. Top them up with cheaper items that you can get away with. For example, there's no point in spending a fortune on sweaters, T-shirts and everyday trousers and skirts. There are plenty of great and cheap places to shop and you can even visit eBay (www.ebay.co.uk) and try to get designer clothes or high street stuff cheaply.

The other top rule is to make sure that you have great shoes. And polished ones at that! It's an old cliché but you are judged by the shoes you wear so anything too wacky and people might think you have a weird shoe fetish (fine if you do and you don't care who knows it of course). Girls, make sure your handbag is a good quality one and not overstuffed. Also, have a pen and a notebook somewhere near the top otherwise when you're out to impress you might end up spending half an hour burrowing around looking for one and your success quota will plummet by 100 points. Sort through your handbag at least once a week as it's surprising how much we can manage to accumulate. I once found myself carrying a harmonica and a book called *Absolute Beginners: Harmonica* in my bag for a whole week. Hardly useful everyday items!

Idea 37 – **Dressing for success**

Your hands are important, so make sure that your nails are well cared for. Treat yourself to a manicure once a month if you can afford it, but at the very least, short, clean nails are a must. Just a word about make-up – don't overdo it! When you're running out of inspiration, approach the make-up counter at your local department store and they'll give you a new look for free. My personal favourite is the Aveda (www.aveda.com) counter as they're good at giving customers a natural look rather than leaving them with a ginger tan.

For more ideas for feeling great and meaning it look at IDEA 41, Soaring self-esteem.

Try another idea...

If you don't know what suits you in terms of colours, you could locate your local rep for Color Me Beautiful (www.colormebeautiful.com or www.cmb.co.uk). You don't have to follow all their suggestions, but having a vague idea of what suits you might prevent you from making expensive mistakes. You might also be able to pick up a couple of tips on how to dress for success from the BBC: www.bbc.co.uk/lifestyle/style/whattowear/.

It's worth buying one or two really good pairs of beautifully cut trousers. My personal favourite for trousers is DAKS (www.daks.com) who know a thing or two about cutting for the fuller bottom. Guys, don't be tempted to buy a cheap suit. You should have at least one suit that makes you feel great and that you're proud of. My personal favourite for blokes suits is Paul Smith (www.paulsmith.co.uk), but anything of good quality that makes you feel good is fine, just so long as it isn't shiny.

'Less is more.'
LUDWIG MIES VAN DER ROHE

Defining idea...

How did it go?

Q **How can I show my personality? Won't I just look like everyone else?**

A Accessorise, accessorise, accessorise! It's definitely worth splashing out on something a little unusual like a wonderful necklace or a funky scarf. Never try to get away with a cheap scarf.

Q **We're allowed to wear what we like to work. I like my belly top so why shouldn't I wear it?**

A First you must judge for yourself the type of environment you work in, and blend in appropriately. If you work in a law office the dress code is obviously going to be an entirely different story to working in a TV studio where a more relaxed style might be more acceptable. I still stand by my original rant against belly tops though. I reckon there's plenty of scope to be all you are when you're on your own time. Anyway, you might want to hold a little bit of you back rather than let all and sundry know everything about you. Create a wee bit of mystery.

Look at the people who really want to make a success of their careers. Not a belly top in sight I bet, regardless of whether they're a lawyer or in the media industry.

38
Design your life to work for you

Sometimes it's not the most talented, gifted or exceptional people that reach the top. So, what's stopping us?

Have you ever wondered how boring old Carruthers got to be company president, yet you're still in the postroom sorting his mail despite the same education, a more charming disposition, more talent at maths and being better looking?

The difference between you and him, my friend, is the way you think. Carruthers knew what he wanted and was prepared to go for it. But do you know where you're going or are you simply floating around in a small boat without a rudder on the sea of 'I haven't got a clue'?

Here's an idea for you...

If a goal appears to be too big and intimidating to tackle, resist the temptation to run away and hide and instead try to break it into bite-sized chunks. First look at the whole huge scary dream and do a five-year vision, based on where you dream of being. Do you see yourself in that corner office on Wall Street or relaxing on the beach with your two kids? If you fancy the latter, you'd better get yourself into gear and start earning more money. Ask yourself what you need to do to achieve that. Can you earn more in your present job? Do you need to change jobs? Should you start your own company? Once you've figured out what you need to do to achieve your big goal, list just one thing you could do today to get there, however small.

SORTING YOU OUT

When the famous industrialist Andrew Carnegie set Napoleon Hill the task of finding out what made successful people successful, Napoleon found out a few vital top secrets from all the hundreds of successful people he interviewed. One of these jewels was that you have to be definite in your purpose or you don't get to your destination. Definiteness of purpose is just another way of saying goal setting – know where you're going and make a plan to achieve it! In the great man's own words: 'We live in a world of overabundance and everything the heart could desire, with nothing standing between us and our desires, excepting lack of a definite purpose.'

Most people will have heard the story about the Harvard University Class of 1954 where they measured those who had set goals against those who had failed to. Those that had set goals ended up much richer, far happier and with more free time.

Idea 38 – **Design your life to work for you**

Go and get a pen and paper right now and start listing the things you want to do or have. You must be specific when you write down your goals. If, for example, you want a car, then specify what type of car you want or you might end up with an old banger (if that's what you do want, then be my guest). Next, set a time when you want to have achieved each thing by and, finally, make a plan of how you might achieve this. This is natural territory for a life coach – it's powerful stuff but only if you get it off the page and start doing it folks! Having someone to spur you along is a great way of ensuring that goals are ticked off.

Visualisation is a powerful way to reinforce goals and it can sometimes produce some astounding results. Many years ago, I was between apartments and wanted somewhere big in a great, central location, with very little rent to pay. Highly unlikely! However, the next day a friend of mine left a message asking whether I knew anyone who wanted to look after a two-bedroom flat right in the part of town I'd had my mind on. I paid very little for it too.

> **If this chapter's grabbed you check out IDEA 42, *Use your imagination*. Also look at IDEA 43, *Working your purpose out*.**

Try another idea...

> **'What the mind of man can conceive and believe it can achieve.'**
> NAPOLEON HILL

Defining idea...

> **'Nothing happens unless first a dream.'**
> CARL SANDBURG

Defining idea...

167

How did it go?

Q I keep meaning to have a goal-setting session, but I never seem to get round to it. I think I'm scared of committing to paper.

A You and the rest of the world! Don't get hung up on worrying whether you have the right goal, just treat it like a brain dump and get anything down on paper even if it's totally impractical. Also, don't try to set all your goals in one session, just have a piece of paper in your pocket and keep adding to it. From skydiving to shark hunting to learning Chinese, leave nothing out just yet and you'll find that the ideas you really want to follow will float to the top like cream on milk. Go after those.

Q I set goals for myself pretty much every New Year's day. I've done this for decades now. How can I move on?

A When companies set financial targets they also set audit dates to run through the figures and see how they're going. Why don't you do the same? We all have New Year resolution lists, but few of us set time limits to achieve them by nor keep a record of them so we can go back and see which ones we can tick off. Sometimes a goal will stay on a list for years. In fact, a friend of mine had 'give up smoking' on her list every year for seven years! She cracked it in the end though and has kept all her past goal lists to gloat over.

39
Effortless balance

If you feel you're working your life away, take stock of your life and do things differently.

Life's usual rigmarole involves getting up and dressed, walking to the bus stop, battling through the crowds, working and then reversing the process. Then it's bed at 9.30 p.m. sharp or you're too tired to function properly the next day.

And what is it all for? To be trapped on the mortgage wheel like a hamster? Let's design you a new life.

MAKE THAT WHEEL WORK FOR YOU

Talking of wheels, a great tool to use in starting to create a life of balance is a 'wheel of life' in order to score your life up and see where you might be out of whack. Get a large sheet of paper and draw a big circle. It doesn't have to be too perfect –

169

Here's an idea for you...

Designing your dream plan will require a lot of time and thought so book a few days off work to take stock of things. If possible, go somewhere nurturing and restful. If you go on a long walk by the beach (or wherever), then take a pen and paper to take notes. If you have a partner, involve them in your 'Get a life' mini-break and establish whether you share the same dreams. For example, you might have visions of living in New York whereas they want to be near their parents in England. So, keep your other half fully immersed in this exciting journey.

apparently, a perfect circle is the first sign of madness! Divide the circle up into eight to twelve sections, like the spokes of a wheel. Allot each section an area of your life such as Relationships, Careers, Social, Health, Spiritual, Family, Dreams, Experiences, Aspirations, Leisure & Recreation, Self-development & Education, Attitude and Financial. Choose the ones that grab you! Give the sections a score out of 10 by assuming that 10 is perfect and lies on the outside of the circle and that 0 is a miserably low score and lies in the middle of the circle. (By the way, a great site to find out more about goal setting is www.mindstore.com.) Next join up the dots and your wheel of life should then have an amoeba-shaped splodge in the middle of it. You should now be able to see where your life is out of balance.

Take two or three of the low scorers off and start setting some goals in those areas. However, before you start setting goals, visualise the big picture first and decide where you're heading. What would be the ideal? Working in a farmhouse in the south of France from your laptop? Next, start making a list of goals on your path to

Idea 39 - **Effortless balance**

achieving this big dream, even if it's only one small goal at a time. Do one thing a day towards your dreams. For example, if the dream was to go and live in France, do your research and get a brochure about houses in the south of France, and use the web to find out about job opportunities out there. You might find out in doing all this that your goals change and evolve but at least you'll know that you've looked into them before rejecting them. The aim of the game is to have no regrets on arrival at the Pearly Gates.

For more on goal setting, IDEA 38, Design your life to work for you, is a must-read.

Try another idea...

Before you start anything, however, do your integrity list. An integrity list is really a deck-clearing exercise. Make a list of the day-to-day things that affect your life such as your environment, your health, your emotions, your finances and your personal relationships. Within these sections, make a list of all the outstanding areas that you haven't given attention to and make a timescale to resolve them. For example, do you save 10% of your earnings? Have you made a will? Are you in credit? Have you found a way to get out of debt and made a plan for it? Once you've started through this list and cleared all those annoying areas that hold you back, you're ready to carry out your *big* dream plan.

> **'Things do not change; we change.'**
> HENRY DAVID THOREAU

Defining idea...

171

How did it go? **Q** **I had so many low scores on my wheel of life, Where do I start?**

A Use your instinct on this one. Which section leaps out at you? The most common areas that need sorting are relationships and career. So, start here if either one is on your list. It's more about actually starting the process than which areas to kick off with. Don't procrastinate and put this off any longer because your dreams can't wait forever.

Q **I realise that work is part of the problem, but I simply don't have the time or money to book a mini-break. Any ideas?**

A Sure, a mini-break doesn't have to mean spending time or money on getting away. It could simply mean setting aside an hour or two in the evening just for you. Or perhaps it could mean making the effort to take your sandwiches away from the desk at lunchtime and going to the park for an hour instead. It might mean arranging for someone else to take care of the kids despite being at home; it might involve telling loved ones and work colleagues that you're not to be disturbed; and it certainly means taking your phone off the hook. Set aside that precious time and use it to calm down and take stock.

40
Clutter busting

Spare room full of dusty boxes and your cupboards stuffed with, well, stuff? Are there things lurking about in your loft that you don't want to know about?

What you're holding onto is old energy. Everything has resonance, meaning a kind of memory — you only have to look at old photos to experience the huge spectrum of emotions that memories can stir up.

Sometimes the emotions are happy and positive, but more often than not, we look back with regret. We wonder if things could have been different, wish that we were younger and healthier, or that we hadn't lost touch with the other people in the photo. We're transported back to the 'then' and therefore we're certainly not in the 'now'. In other words, we're trapped by our past with no room for our future. This is a very unhealthy state of mind and doesn't make for a true picture of holistic wellbeing.

I knew an eccentric old lady who *never* threw anything away. Her collection of supermarket plastic bags was legendary. Nothing, not a bus ticket, not a single old

> **Here's an idea for you...**
>
> Consider renting space (anything from the size of a crate to the size of house) from a storage company such as U-Haul (www.uhaul.com). Size up the clutter you think you can get rid of, then rent the equivalent storage space. Choose a company that offers relatively short-term rentals for, say, three months. Not only will you get all that stuff out of your house, you'll also get to ask yourself whether you missed anything when your contract expires. If you didn't, perhaps now's the time to bin it. If you're still hesitating, renew for another three months if you think it's worth the money.

bill, not even a wonky, old, broken radio was consigned to the bin. And you know what? She never achieved anything in her life. All her dreams remained just dreams because all those heavy memories held her back and she became pinned down by all the responsibility of 'looking after' all that rubbish. What she was saying to herself and to the universe was probably, 'I'll never have the resources in my life to have enough, therefore I'll just hold on to what I've got.'

Memories are, of course, important and it's great to look back on the good old days, but not to the point of sentimentality. There comes a time when the only way to move forward is to let go of the things that are holding you back. It's a law of nature that as soon as you get rid of stuff, more stuff comes into your life to replace it. So, don't panic, as clearing clutter is a lifetime's work!

CLUTTER CLEAROUTS

Getting started is always the trickiest part and the only way to do it is to start on a small scale. Don't try to declutter the whole house in one go. As the old saying goes, 'If you want to eat an elephant, don't use a teaspoon.' Get your diary out, allocate

Idea 40 – **Clutter busting**

two or three hours of your time and then select your target. Start with something small like a cupboard. Keep asking yourself when the last time was that you used or thought about the items you come across. Set a limit of three months and if you haven't thought about, used or missed something over the last three months then bin it. The rules of engagement are: Chuck it, file it, delegate it or do something about it. Don't just rearrange the cupboard and put everything back in again. What a waste of your time that would be! Of course, when I say chuck it you can always give it away, take it to a charity shop or sell it. But for goodness sake don't get stuck in the small print, meaning that sometimes a sale or trip to a charity shop can take too much time and effort to organise and bin bags might simply sit in the hall for six months. Get prepared for your great throw-out day. Nowadays there are plenty of cheap storage solutions – boxes, files, desks, etc. Be sure to get enough bin bags and boxes and find out where your local dump is. Get to the point of organisation where you know you can't wriggle out of this commitment to yourself.

Try another idea... **For more on getting your act together see IDEA 38, *Design your life to work for you*, or IDEA 39, *Effortless balance*.**

On the great day itself, start at the time that you've allotted in your diary. Don't aim to try to finish everything, just do however much you can do in the time you've allowed. Make sure you have at least a month's worth of dates scheduled in for decluttering. This is a great project to work on with a life coach, as they will hold you to it. And boy will you feel better when it's done! Organised, efficient, clear-headed and free!

Defining idea... **'Three rules of work: out of clutter find simplicity; from discord find harmony; in the middle of difficulty lies opportunity.'**
ALBERT EINSTEIN

52 Brilliant Ideas – **Get healthy for good**

How did it go?

Q   What if I throw something away then realise I need it?

A   This is exactly why you should try a halfway house approach like rented storage first. Instead of binning something right off, put it out of sight for a while and give yourself some time to think clearly about whether or not you need it.

Q   I like the idea of rented storage, but I don't have the cash to do it. How else can I try the halfway house approach?

A   Do any of your friends and family have boxes full of junk? More than likely. So, why don't you suggest that you do a junk swap for three months? This will mean that you both get to clear stuff out of your respective houses and be given the opportunity to see if you miss anything. I bet you'll have some fun reminiscing about the old days in the process!

176

41
Soaring self-esteem

We formulate who we are through a lifetime of experience. As children, our self-confidence is either nurtured or destroyed depending on how we interpret events.

I have a friend whose view of men was coloured by her experiences as a five-year-old child.

When on holiday with her parents at the seaside, she formed a play friendship with an older boy who was a skilled sandcastle builder. At the end of the day, having been a very willing assistant to the boy's efforts, my friend thought she deserved at least a kiss. Unsurprisingly the boy wasn't into kissing girls and told her this in no uncertain terms! The sense of rejection she felt has haunted my friend throughout her life. The interpretation she put on this tiny event was that men would reject her.

Unless you have very forward-thinking and sensitive parents who are ready to reinterpret these messages, hundreds of assumptions are formed before we reach

Here's an idea for you...

Get some perspective and start looking up rather than down! I mean this literally. Stop spending so much of your time thinking about the past and future and looking down at your boots. Spend a day looking up instead and see how much more positive you feel about life. Look at your body and how you're holding yourself. Stop slouching otherwise you'll feel like a slouch. Stand up tall, put your shoulders back and smile. Acting as if you were confident will work quickly and effectively to elevate your self-esteem.

Defining idea...

'Drag your thoughts away from your troubles...by the ears, by the heels, or any other way you can manage it.'
MARK TWAIN

adulthood. A teacher could have told you that you'll never amount to anything in your life, or your first boyfriend could have told you that you're fat. The trick is to know that everyone is filtering the 'truth'. In other words, everyone is wearing different, funny-coloured pairs of spectacles and seeing their own version of the truth.

FULL HOUSE

Getting your own house in order first is the key to self-esteem. Knowing the boundaries of what you will and won't accept is vital. In this way, those around you aren't defining who you are the whole time. If you went by their reflections, you would never know who you're trying to be. You can't please everyone all of the time. The only thing you can do is do the best for yourself and know where your limits are.

Idea 41 – **Soaring self-esteem**

WILL-O'-THE-WISP

Self-confidence is a will-o'-the-wisp that can disappear as fast as you've captured it. The trick is to build on your esteem foundations so that you can refer to your successes and know that you have a core of confidence that will never be knocked. Start building up your own library of successes in your life, from when you won the Tennis Improvement Cup to getting into university. If you can put these mementos into a scrapbook, great. Collect photos and certificates of your glorious moments so that you then have a permanent record of wins that you can go back and refer to, no matter how bad things get in the future.

*For other great ideas on this look at IDEA 43, **Working your purpose out**, and IDEA 38, **Design your life to work for you**.*

Try another idea...

Q My job is eating away at my self-esteem. What can I do about it?

A Well, you could change jobs, but your self-esteem might be too low to look at this option just yet. You need to change your attitude. If there's a particular person getting you down then change your attitude towards them. Instead of hating them, make an effort to be extra helpful and extra nice. Go the extra mile! Disarm them with your charm! Pretend that you're confident, even if you're not. Everyone is doing this and people who come across as confident generally feel they don't have a clue what they're doing and are terrified of being found out!

How did it go?

Q **My partner is always putting me down and when this happens I really feel my confidence hitting the floor. What can I do to stop it?**

A Look at your boundaries. It's very important to know where you begin and your partner ends. Perfect partnerships are about being a team and each team member has something unique to contribute. If everybody did the same thing in the same way, we wouldn't get very far. I'd suggest becoming gently assertive, which isn't the same as being aggressive. Being assertive is knowing what your needs are and gently getting them. The biggest word in an assertive person's vocabulary is 'No.'

Q **Who can give me self-confidence? Is it something I can pay someone to help me build?**

A You could work with a life coach, but fundamentally, nobody can give you confidence. You have to believe in yourself, your values and where you stand and don't be swayed by anyone telling you that you can't be an extraordinary human being. As the Buddha said, 'Peace comes from within. Do not seek it without.'

42

Use your imagination

Consider this the instruction manual for the most powerful and underutilised tool you possess. Your brain.

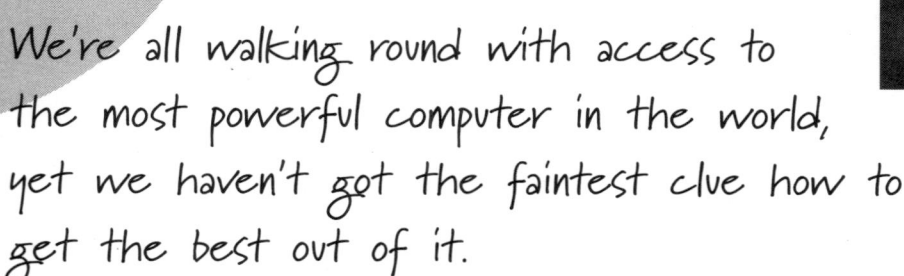

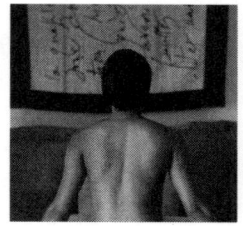

We're all walking round with access to the most powerful computer in the world, yet we haven't got the faintest clue how to get the best out of it.

In the West we try to protect ourselves against life by using logic. We put great emphasis on school subjects like maths, English, science and languages, and imagination and creativity are effectively banned by the age of five. Can anyone remember the shock of going from pre-school to junior school and realising that dipping your hands in paint and scribbling on huge pieces of paper wasn't what was expected from you anymore?

What a leap! There you were happily being creative and being told how clever you were – a genius in fact – all day long by nice teachers when suddenly you had to understand algebra and long division for goodness sake! There's a distinct moment when the new crispy uniform for junior school really doesn't seem worth it. It strikes you like a cold dark hand gripping your insides – a dawning horror that you're going to be doing 'work' for the rest of your life and that crayons are distinctly for the under-5s.

Here's an idea for you... **Sit in a chair, close your eyes and visualise how your day is going to be. Remember, this exercise isn't based on reality but only held back by the confines of your imagination. For example, visualise leaving the house, the pleasant walk to the station, the receptionist's smile or the warm greeting of your spouse on returning home. See if you get a better day by imagining one. This works best when you're going to give a presentation or make an important deal. Practising for an event like this will hone your performance and knock the edge off your nerves.**

I know that some people will go off and be artists when they grow up (the lucky ones?), but parents often greet this job choice with, 'That's not a real job!'

We totally overexercise this logical (left) side of the brain to the massive detriment of our creative (right) side, which is also responsible for intuition. The right side is in effect totally dominated by strong 'left logic' and it takes quite a bit for the right side to get heard. Occasionally we might get a flash of inspiration, a dream, a moment when everything makes sense, but this is rare. The way to balance out this disparity is to start using our imagination again. Exercising this important muscle is vital. Before dismissing this idea as childish, take note that many of the world's great sportsmen are using this technique, which first became popular with the 'Inner Game' books. A proven way to improve your game is to use your imagination to play the shot in your head first, practise in your inner gym and then actually do it in reality. Performance will increase dramatically. It has to. Whether we like it or not those of us who aren't sporting heroes are also using our imagination the whole time, but we're generally picturing disastrous outcomes rather than positive wins. We are, in effect, playing the shot in our heads and programming ourselves for failure.

Idea 42 – Use your imagination

If you could start rehearsing your life in your head, would your 'game' of life improve? Certainly the reverse is true. Bridget Jones' vision of ending up as a lonely old lady devoured by dogs will only come true if that's what you focus on. It's the classic case of the self-fulfilling prophecy.

Check out IDEA 45, *You have one day to live!* – you need to live in the here and now, rather than the now and then.

Try another idea...

If you doubt the power of imagination over your ability to perform, just think about this. If I was to offer £1,000 to anyone prepared to walk a 2-metre plank of wood that I'd placed on the floor, there would be a line of people queuing round the block. Yet if I was to place the same plank 100 metres above ground between two buildings, those same people would be phoning the funny farm to have me taken away. The difference between the two walks is that the latter summons up pictures of the strawberry-jam consequences of splatting on the pavement, which is enough to stymie your chances of success.

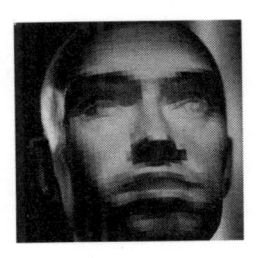

'Imagination is more important than knowledge.'
ALBERT EINSTEIN

Defining idea...

183

How did it go?

Q **I can't visualise. When I close my eyes, all I can see is a great big black hole. What am I supposed to see?**

A   *Don't worry. You don't actually have to see anything. You might simply feel or hear things when you close your eyes and use your imagination. That's totally cool.*

Q **I'm an accountant and I'm not sure that my imagination muscle is still functioning. What can I do?**

A   *Close your eyes and 'see' the room you are sitting in – can you do that? Now close your eyes once more and imagine the journey to work, closing the front door, walking to the station, catching the train. Easy? You already have a great imagination. Now all you have to do is use it!*

Idea 42 – **Use your imagination**

185

52 Brilliant Ideas – **Get healthy for good**

43
Working your purpose out

**My particular purpose in life is lifting your game.
What's yours?**

You get out of bed, put the cereal in the toaster and the milk on the toast, and pat the wife and kiss the dog as you leave for work. You have a dark suspicion lurking deep within you. Is this it? Is this all I can expect?

You don't have to be a slave to your job. But knowing what you don't want to do is the easy part of the equation. The tough bit is deciding just what would make you happy. Working with a life coach is a great way to force yourself to face these big questions head on.

Coaching is a relatively new concept that has exploded into quite a movement over the last five years, to the point where in certain circles everyone who is anyone is working with a coach. Coaching shouldn't be confused with mentoring. A mentor is someone who is, for example, a leader in your field who will tell you how to avoid pitfalls and to avoid making the same mistakes as they did. A coach, on the other

> **Here's an idea for you...**
>
> Ask yourself what you really enjoy doing, and then think about ways to make this activity more central to your life. See how the professionals do this at www.laurabermanfortgang.com and at www.fionaharrold.com.

hand, doesn't 'tell' you to do anything. Coaching works by asking you the right questions so that you can find the answer yourself. As the saying goes, 'Give a man a fish he eats for a day but teach him how to fish and you feed him for life.' There's no point in a coach telling you what to do unless you want to live the coach's life and not your own. Coaching isn't a counselling process either. It assumes that you're healthy in mind and ready to move on from your past and into your future.

You might think that you have lots of friends who could do the same job as a coach but for free, but remember that all of your friends have a vested interest in keeping you just where you are now. They won't usually want you to move on as they like you just the way you are, plus you might show them up for being stuck where they are. Imagine that you tell your best mate that you're considering starting a new life in Spain. 'Oh', he says, 'I heard a story once about someone moving to Spain that would make your hair curl...' And before you know it you've retreated under your own personal rain cloud.

Laura Berman Fortgang, a coach from the US, talks about finding your essence. Finding your essence means finding a nugget of passion in you that might grow into an ingot of gold. Laura was an actress desperately seeking success. The essence she mined, which ultimately led her to be a professional life coach, was that she loved getting up and performing (which she does now in coaching). Also, she loved

Idea 43 – **Working your purpose out**

understanding people and their motivation (again, she now does this in coaching). Although she wasn't successful as an actress, she found that coaching had many similar roots to acting.

Believe in yourself – check into IDEA 41, *Soaring self-esteem*.

Try another idea...

Your clues to your future are in your past. My brother was lucky to find his essence early on. He loved aeroplanes as a kid and would always be scouring the skies identifying types. He was passionate about making model planes from kits and my dad encouraged him all the way. My brother went on to become the aviation editor for a huge specialist magazine and is now a novelist writing about the obvious. You guessed it, planes. Look for your essence in the hobbies and activities that you do in your free time and especially in the careers that you abandoned for being impractical. Start putting together a list of all your passions and establish why you're so enthusiastic about them. Let's say you loved catching bugs and putting them in matchboxes as a child. What turned you on? Was it being outside? Was it collecting something? Was it the intellectual discipline of collecting bugs of one species? Keep digging until you find that nugget. Don't abandon your dream to play a small game. Play a huge game instead. What have you got to lose?

'Our deepest fear isn't that we are inadequate. Our deepest fear is that we are powerful beyond measure. It is our light, not our darkness that frightens us.'
NELSON MANDELA, 1994 inaugural speech

Defining idea...

189

52 Brilliant Ideas – **Get healthy for good**

How did it go?

Q **How do I find a life coach to suit my needs?**

A Have a look at the International Coach Federation's website (www.coachfederation.org). This organisation will give you information about coaching, coaching courses and coaches. Most coaches will give you a free session to enable you to see if they're your particular cup of tea. Vote with your feet! If you don't like the feel of them go on looking until you find someone you'd like to work with. Of course, personal recommendations are always best.

Q **I had a session with a life coach and didn't hit it off with her. How do I know whether this is personal or whether I'm actually rejecting the idea of advice from an outsider?**

A Try another coach to find out whether it was the person not the approach that didn't appeal the first time.

44
You're the most important person in your life

The worm has turned! Now it's time to put yourself first.

This isn't as selfish as it might sound. In an aeroplane when the oxygen masks descend, what must you do? Put your own mask on first and then help others. The fact is, if you're not looking after yourself you're in no position to look after others.

By the way, do they ever actually use those oxygen masks on planes? Or is the threat of them being needed just a way of freaking out nervous passengers? Just one more thing to think about.

The first place to start in terms of putting yourself first is to establish where your own personal boundaries lie. By this I mean where and how you personally know when someone else is taking the micky. For example, a friend goes away and asks you to call round and water her plants, look after the goldfish and feed the cat

> **Here's an idea for you...**
>
> Book out an entire day to do exactly what you want (within the boundaries of the law, obviously). Plan your day meticulously, as if you're doing it for someone else. What would you like to do? Go to an art gallery? Check into a health spa for the day? Go to the zoo? Have a long bath then go to bed with a good book? Make space for yourself in your life. You need this space to be yourself, to be creative, to be regenerated. Don't feel guilty about it. Enjoy!

(maybe you could combine these last two activities!). You're really cheesed off about this because this particular 'friend' is always asking you to do this kind of thing, but never returns the favour. You don't say anything, however, in case you upset her. All you do is complain to your friends, which isn't going to solve the problem. Knowing your boundaries is being able to say 'No' because you know what you want and which direction you're heading to in your life. Saying 'No' is an art form, but you don't have to suddenly become Mr or Mrs Horrible. The trick is not to volunteer in the first place.

Let me give you an example. Your friend comes by and mentions that he has to hand in a report by Monday only his printer is broken. You notice that the report isn't in the right format and that it's over a thousand pages long but before you can stop yourself you say nicely, 'I'll do all the corrections and print it out for you on my printer.' Your friend thanks you, dumps the report on you and heads out for the pub, leaving you to spend the only sunny Saturday of the year inside doing your friend's work, which he should have done correctly in the first place. You're fuming.

Idea 44 – You're the most important person in your life

Right. Let's re-run that scene. Your friend comes by and mentions that he has to finish his report by Monday only his printer is broken. You zip your lip. And in case you think you're being nasty, you have *your* life to live, not someone else's. Your friend is over twenty-one and you must trust him to come up with the solution. You have plans too, you know.

> **For more on creating space and time for yourself see IDEA 49, *Space invaders*.**
>
> *Try another idea...*

Another trick that will both carve yourself time and make yourself the most important person in your life is to schedule. Put your time down in your diary and stick to it. Your diary should consist of appointments that you have to do at a certain time (e.g. your weekly sales meeting), appointments that don't have to be done at a specific time (e.g. the meeting with the personnel manager to talk over various staffing issues) and appointments that don't have to be done at any specific time. That's where you start scheduling. Put your holidays in your diary *now*. Put down the trip to the beach *now*. The same goes with your son's nativity play or your gym sessions. Prioritise yourself *now*. And if, for instance, you book in half a day's holiday to go to your wife's graduation and the sales director for the whole of the world market rings and asks if you can have a meeting that afternoon say, 'No, but I could make Friday morning.' 'Fine,' he'll reply. It really is that simple, you just have to hold your nerve.

> *'I want to be alone!'*
> GRETA GARBO
>
> *Defining idea...*

193

52 Brilliant Ideas – **Get healthy for good**

How did it go?

Q **A friend of mine would often ask me to look after her cat, goldfish and plants, but she hasn't been round to see me so much recently. Is this a sign that I'm losing all my friends?**

A Are you really sure that this character was your friend? Stick around people who are going to nurture you, not ones who steal all your energy.

Q **How can I rid this feeling of guilt about saying 'No'?**

A If you don't know where you're going, someone else will and they'll use you to help them achieve their ambitions. Don't let them. Instead of being programmed, start programming yourself by choosing activities and people who will actually help you on your life's journey.

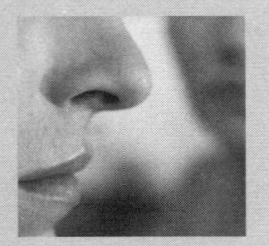

194

45
You have one day to live!

We undermine our health every day by not living in the present. Why spend all your time worrying about what might have been or what might happen tomorrow?

Have you ever driven somewhere and simply arrived as if by magic? We can become so engrossed in our thinking that we can unwittingly put the operation of our lives on automatic pilot.

Imagine you're at the doctors waiting for your test results. The door swings opens and the doctor sits you down and says, 'I'm afraid the news is bad – you only have a year to live.' What would you do with that year? Who would you become? Would you go out and help run a soup kitchen? Would you go round the world? Would you spend all your money?

This actually happened to my Uncle Tone who had his fortune told by a gypsy who said he would die when he was forty years old. So, he blew all his money on everything in sight, including a very fetching moleskin suit. However, unfortunately, or should I say fortunately, he survived another twenty years, but with a lot less money.

MIND MATTERS

Mind control is everything. You are who you think you are (it took me a while to work that one out too). A good starting point is to accept that you can't change the past, however much you might want to. You can forgive the past and move on, but I'm afraid that without H. G. Wells and his time machine, you're stuck in the here and now. It might be a New Age trick, but forgiving those who have caused you harm is a place to start. Holding on to resentment and hurt over someone's past deeds is actually causing no damage to them whatsoever. The only person affected by that thinking is you! So stop that right now, forgive them and vow to move on to your future. Talking of the future, that's another favourite place of ours to lurk. Worrying about it is a great way to freak us out completely. What if we lose our job, don't have enough money to pay the mortgage, get thrown out of our house and have to beg for scraps of food? I personally frequently imagine something terrible happening to some family member and then imagine what I'm going to wear at the funeral. Horrible. And a complete waste of time and a drain on our energy.

Here's an idea for you... Try living today in the present. This won't be as easy as it sounds because thoughts are like chattering monkeys, jumping around from tree to tree. The only time when there's some respite is when we're asleep. Every time you feel yourself worrying about the future say to yourself, 'I'm not going to think about that now.' How does it feel to be right in the here and now?

...and another The Power of Now by Eckhart Tolle (www.eckharttolle.com). I find with these kinds of books that even if you don't agree with all of the content or you find that they've got God a little more than you have, you can always take something useful from it. There will always be a nugget of gold worth mining for.

Idea 45 – **You have one day to live!**

GET A STRATEGY

A must-have in your personal-development library is *How to Stop Worrying and Start Living* by Dale Carnegie. He also wrote the best selling *How to Win Friends and Influence People*. His book is really all you need for developing a strategy to cope with worry. Written just after the Second World War, he really must have known what worry was about. We forget what an unbelievably destabilising influence the war must have had on people's worlds. My mother-in-law was a little girl in London during the Blitz and came back from school to find her house had been blown to bits. Luckily, nobody was killed. However, imagine losing everything, including loved ones. One of Carnegie's tactics is to imagine that your worries are in watertight compartments. In the days when he was writing, ships had mechanical bulkheads that were able to section off parts of the hull should one area develop a leak, thus stopping the whole ship from being overwhelmed with water and sinking. Keep your worries behind the bulkhead and don't let them out again. That way they won't overwhelm or sink you.

I have several strategies for dealing with worry. For instance, I keep a pen and some paper by my bed at all times so that if I wake in the night and start to fret, I can jot my worries down so that I can deal with them the following day. Sometimes, by the time it gets to morning they're no longer anything to worry about. This strategy is like a mind dump and stops everything swilling around in your brain.

Try another idea...

You must check out **IDEA 48, Breathe in, breathe out!**, and **IDEA 49, Space Invaders**.

Defining idea...

'The mountain is there, whether the clouds hide it or not.'
SUFI SAYING

197

My other main strategy involves the news. I don't ever watch the news on TV or read a newspaper. I listen to the news once a day on the radio and that's it. We're totally inundated with images of bad news, woe, fear, gossip, disaster, war, politics and, worse still, politicians! It's a small wonder that we're worried about our future!

How did it go?

Q **I find that I just can't stop thinking. It's driving me nuts! What can I do?**

A The trick isn't to stop thinking but to watch the thoughts and emotions without being pulled in by them.

Q **I'm a total worrier – is there anything I can do to get my worries into perspective?**

A Try imagining the worst thing that could possibly happen. For example, you might think – 'I might lose my job.' Then ask yourself the question 'Then what?' You might think – 'Well I wouldn't be able to live in this house.' 'Then what?' 'Then I'd move.' 'Then what?' 'Then I'd go to a smaller house in a cheaper part of town.' 'Then what?' Keep going until you realise that the worst thing that you can possibly think of isn't actually that bad. You know what? Whatever life throws at you, you'd handle it.

46
Review of the greats

What can these old dogs teach us?

Imagine your gorgeous new girlfriend invites you back for a coffee at her place. While she's in the kitchen, you scour the books in her lounge and notice with horror that they're all self-help books. Is this woman sane or have you found yourself a bunny-boiler?

This new girlfriend is probably the one you should marry! At least she's open enough to find depth in life and she's willing to learn and be humble. Beware the ones who think they know it all! Anyway, in this age of spin, self-help books should be called success tools. Most people feel embarrassed about needing help, but everyone needs help at becoming more successful!

I'VE STARTED SO I'LL FINISH

You don't have to read a self-help cover to cover. Pick only the chapters that either appeal to you or those you feel you particularly need. Also make notes in the margin

Here's an idea for you...

At the centre of most self-help books is positive thinking. So, set yourself a challenge: don't allow yourself any negative thoughts for three hours. When and if a negative thought enters your mind, reset the clock and start again each time.

or you'll never remember what the main message is. Another tip is to have a notebook for summaries of the strategies you're learning. A way to reinforce what you're learning is to see if there are any courses available – sometimes it's easier to take two days out of your life to focus on the subject, rather than try to read the book. My favourite courses are the MindStore courses (www.mindstore.com).

I always try to grab a nugget of truth from each of the self-development books that I've read, however much they differ from my cultural expectations. These range from *The Tibetan Book of Living and Dying* to *Think and Grow Rich*! You'll find that all these books have something that you can take away and use. One of my personal favourites is a guy called Ed Foreman (www.edforeman.com). When I first came across Ed I must say I thought that he was possibly the most annoying person on the planet. But you know what? I'm rather fond of him now. The main reason why I couldn't get on with his philosophy at first was that his Texan drawl and my English sensitivities clashed. Now I just take him for what he is, take the nugget and run!

The other guy I'm particularly fond of is Dale Carnegie. His book, *How to Stop Worrying and Start Living*, is one of the all-time greats, in my opinion. This book was written when the Second World War was fresh in people's minds, which certainly lends perspective when looking at our problems today.

Defining idea...

'Sit quietly, doing nothing, spring comes, and the grass grows by itself.'
ZEN SAYING

*Idea 46 – **Review of the greats***

KEEP ON LEARNING

You'll never know it all and you'll never stop learning. Make it a habit to read something inspirational each morning before you go to work. This will be much better for you than listening to the news.

> You must have a look at IDEA 38, ***Design your life to work for you***, and IDEA 43, ***Working your purpose out.***

TOP TIPS FROM THE TOP

Here is a list of my definitive top 10 success books (in no particular order):

1. Andrew Carnegie – *The Autobiography of Andrew Carnegie* (1920)
2. Stephen R. Covey – *The 7 Habits of Highly Effective People* (1989)
3. Napoleon Hill – *Think and Grow Rich* (1937)
4. Dale Carnegie – *How to Stop Worrying and Start Living*
5. Napoleon Hill and W. Clement Stone – *Success Through a Positive Mental Attitude* (1960)
6. Nelson Mandela – *Long Walk to Freedom: The Autobiography of Nelson Mandela* (1994)
7. Cheryl Richardson – *Take Time for Your Life: A Seven-Step Programme for Creating the Life You Want* (1998)
8. Anthony Robbins – *Unlimited Power: The New Science of Personal Achievement* (1986)
9. Laura Berman Fortgang – *Living Your Best Life Yet*
10. Zig Ziglar – *See You at the Top* (1975)

How did it go?

Q **There are so many self-help books out there! How do I start to choose?**

A   I'd suggest that you begin at the beginning. Start with Napoleon Hill's book Think and Grow Rich. Readers find the title a challenge because to be openly out for the money is simply not playing with a straight bat. See past the title, however, and remember that the book was written in 1937 when the world was a very different place and the Great Depression had brought people to their knees. Even better than the books are the tapes that are recorded by Nightingale Conant (www.nightingale.com). Try Napoleon Hill's The Science of Personal Achievement.

Q **How do I get enough time to read all these books?**

A   Again, tapes and CDs are the way forward here. Use your morning commute to improve your soul! Or 'improve' to the hoovering.

Q **This self-help lark could cost a fortune!**

A   Remember that you can always request books at your library, rather than dish out loads of cash. Two great books that summarise the top self-help books are Tom Butler-Bowdon's 50 Success Classics and 50 Self Help Classics. These will show you what you're getting into before you commit to buying anything. I do self-help book swaps with friends.

47

Daily habits

It's the things that we do every day that kill us.

If we had just the occasional drink and cigarette a month our bodies would probably cope. However, twenty a day and a bottle of wine each night will do us in eventually. What if each day we were to do small, positive things to enhance our health instead?

HABITS MAKETH MAN

Habits make or break us. Twenty years ago I remember looking at a friend of mine and admiring his discipline, tenacity and drive. Twenty years later, he's got it all – a lovely wife, a gorgeously huge home, perfect dogs and kids, and a summer place abroad. He's strong, fit, healthy and, what's more, he's a really nice guy. Don't you just hate him? Habits have made him and have included getting up early, exercising,

Here's an idea for you... **List all the positive habits that you'd like to incorporate into your life, which might range from walking the dog to quitting the weed! Then add in just one new habit a week. Start with an easy one first, such as getting up 10 minutes earlier each day. Then the following week add another, like 10 minutes of stretching. Tick off each habit as you incorporate it into your schedule and once you've done four, give yourself a small reward like a facial or a trip somewhere nice. The following month add another four new habits, and so on.**

not smoking or drinking to excess and having a calm mind every single day. We all have mates who have gone down the other road, which was classed as the much cooler road when we were younger. This is the getting trollied road and the doing no exercise road. The trouble is, if you take this road you're likely to wake up at 45 years old, fat, drunk and stupid and that's no way to go through life. You'll pay for that 'animal house' philosophy in the end, however boring it might be in the short term.

INSIST ON INSPIRATION

One of my personal favourites in terms of hints regarding good habits is Ed Foreman. You can buy his tapes from a company called Nightingale Connant (www.nightingale.com) that specialises in self-development audio programmes. You'll need to get over his Texan drawl first though! He has a 'Terrific' Day Menu on his website (www.edforeman.com) that includes getting up early, reading something uplifting, going for an early morning walk and doing stretching exercises. In the morning listen to something inspirational rather than to what I call the Morning Misery Guts Programme (the early morning news analysis programme) that tends to be on. This programme is supposed to set you up for the day, but in my view it's depressing stuff. Before ten to seven in the morning the presenters have usually had several huge rows with squirming politicians, updated you on the day's wars and murders, and warned you that you might be blown up on the way to work by all the mad people out to get you! Go one step further and throw away your telly – turf it out of your life. You'll get masses more time for all those habits that you keep saying you have no time to develop. When I junked the TV about ten years ago, I thought that the programme *ER* (Emergency Room apparently) was a programme about our Queen (Elizabeth Regina). How wrong I was! So, don't ditch the box if you want to keep up with the gossip.

New Age business guru Stephen R. Covey shows he knows the value of habits in his 1990 bestseller *The 7 Habits of Highly Effective People*. It might be worth a visit to www.getinthehabit.com where you can buy the book and join the forum for those that follow his habits. Remember that successful people are only successful because they have spent less time in the pub talking about being rich and famous and more time actually doing something about it!

It's difficult to have good habits if your home is one big junk yard – do your mind a favour and look at IDEA 40, *Clutter busting*.

Try another idea...

'We are what we repeatedly do.'
ARISTOTLE

Defining idea...

How did it go?

Q **I find I start well, but after a few weeks I forget about my new good habit. Any suggestions?**

A *First of all, don't beat yourself up about it. It happens to us all. It's very difficult to change habits, especially to rid ourselves of the bad ones, which love to come creeping back. Quite simply, start again and don't give up until the habit becomes part of you.*

Q **This is all very well, but many of my daily bad habits (after-work drinks, choc-fests, etc.) are down to my friends and family. Do I have to avoid them now?**

A *Unless you're in solitary confinement then the behaviour of other people is always going to affect your own routine. This means that you may have to incorporate friends and family into your plans. Instead of trying to duck out of old habits (which may make it look like you're shunning other people), try calling a 'habit summit' and explaining what and why you'd like to change. You may be surprised to find that others want to change too.*

Idea 47 – **Daily habits**

52 Brilliant Ideas – **Get healthy for good**

48 Breathe in, breathe out!

Proper breathing can be a forgotten art for people in stressful jobs, lives or relationships. And these days we often hold onto our breath out of sheer terror.

It's not called the life breath for nothing. With each breath we exchange carbon dioxide from inside the body with life-giving oxygen from outside. If this incredible process was interrupted for more than a few minutes, it would be curtains.

The partner to breathing is an amazingly reliable muscle: your heart. Oxygen-rich blood is pumped by the heart from the lungs via the arteries and small capillaries to all the cells of the body. This allows the cells to function. Carbon dioxide is then transported back to the heart through the veins and from there it's pumped to the lungs and we breathe it out. The whole process starts again with our next in-breath. Breathing is an amazing, miraculous process and it's worked so well that it hasn't changed one iota since we were running away from sabre-toothed beasties. Sometimes, however, that's just the problem.

Here's an idea for you...

When you're at the office, why not make your company's toilet your personal breathing booth?

We may think that we're civilised humans who know the difference between Armani and Woolworths, but the fact is that as far as our ancient intuitive response mechanisms go, we're just another animal fighting for our tiny space in the (concrete) jungle. We humans go through the same physiological reaction as a cat does when it's dumped in a barrel of freezing water or being chased by a dog, or as a mouse does when a cat is stalking it for that matter. When faced with what we perceive as a danger (this could be your tax bill, your boss or being late for work), we go into a state of hyperarousal known as the flight-or-fight system. You might think that hyperarousal sounds a bit saucy, but it actually means feelings like anxiety, rage or sheer blind terror. The resulting flight-or-fight mechanism is unbelievably clever and causes a rapid cascade of nervous-system firings and the release of powerful hormones like adrenaline. We become hyperaware of all our surroundings, the pupils of our eyes dilate to let in more light, the hair on our body stands up so that we become more sensitive to vibrations, the digestive system shuts down and the heart rate shoots up so that there's more blood available for legging it up a tree at top speed. And that's just for starters! Here's the technical part – you've just activated the sympathetic part of your autonomic nervous system. Impress your friends with that one!

This brings us back to breathing. Breathing centres you. It's almost impossible to be stressed if breathing is measured, calm and deep. Breathing overrides the powerful stress response and slows down the reaction of the autonomic nervous system. So, the good news is that you have some degree of control over how you react to stress.

BREATHING EXERCISES

Breathing exercises are deceptively simple and dynamically powerful. All you need is a few minutes a day to provide you with a powerful way of dealing with stress. There are hundreds of different exercises you could do. I'm going to give you just two for starters. Do them! Don't just read this and think it's for someone else. It's for you. It's for us all!

Exercise 1: observing the breath

Sit on a comfortable chair, making sure that your feet are on the ground. Close your eyes, rest one hand in your lap and place the other on your tummy. You should feel the tummy expanding as you breathe in and contracting as you breathe out. Breathe in deeply through your nose and silently count 'one'. Breathe out. Breathe in again and count 'two'. Do this for up to 10 breaths and then do it the other way round. Breathe in. Breathe *out* and count 'one'. Breathe in. Breathe out and count 'two'. Do this for five rounds to start with, building up to 10. Do this once a day.

Exercise 2: anti-stress breath

Try this if you find yourself stressed out and in need of some immediate relief. Breathe in for four counts, hold for four counts and exhale for four counts. Remember to let the out-breath out slowly, not in a rush. Do this for about five cycles, being careful that you don't overdo it otherwise you could end up feeling a bit dizzy.

Try another idea...

To see what else you can do to relieve stress, check out IDEA 4, **Stressed out.**

Defining idea...

'**Get wisdom and rest in peace.**'
SIVANANDA, the historical Buddha

52 Brilliant Ideas – **Get healthy for good**

How did it go?

Q **I keep meaning to do the exercises because I know they'll be great and I'll really feel the difference, but I keep forgetting to do them.**

A Put the breathing exercises in your diary initially and write reminders on sticky notes on your bathroom mirror. It takes around 21 days to form a habit, but once you're into it, the habit will stick.

Q **How else can I make breathing a habit?**

A Try tapes – I find that meditation tapes are great for breathing exercises. There can be long silences, so don't let the guiding voice on the tape make you jump out of your skin when they start talking again! Try Andrew Weil's tape, Breathing – The Masterkey to Self Healing.

49

Space invaders

Find the space for your mind and meditate on a daily basis.

How many books on meditation do you own? Whether it's twenty-five or none, neither approach will actually get you meditating. The former is only useful if you plan to open a library and doing nothing won't get you anywhere.

We're subject to hundreds of stimuli every day and our reaction to these stimuli can constitute stress. However, we all know that an event we perceive stressful may not be perceived as stressful to someone else in the same situation. Dr Hans Selye first coined the term 'stress' in the 1950s and it has quickly become an umbrella term for many of the various pressures we experience in life. Some stressors (an event that produces the stress response) are unavoidable, like gravity or exposure to toxic chemicals, whilst others are purely down to perception – in other words, how you see things will determine how much stress you'll experience. We therefore need to somehow see events differently, through a different pair of glasses. Rose-tinted ones are my personal favourite.

Here's an idea for you...

As an alternative to your own script, get a pre-recorded meditation. Amazon have a good selection. You could try your local Buddhist centre – they're not usually out to convert you, but for the sceptics amongst you there are also plenty of secular options. I know I said throw away the books, but consider *Full Catastrophe Living* by Jon Kabat-Zinn, which also comes on tape.

Calming the mind down from stressful thoughts is a powerful way to regain control of uncontrollable events that you could therefore feel anxious about. Meditation has been seen by many as Eastern mystical claptrap. In fact, meditation got bad press many years ago, as sceptics thought that while there were no thoughts in the mind the devil could nip in and take over. However, if you've ever actually tried to empty your mind for a moment, you'll have realised that it's virtually impossible, at least for any length of time. Meditation isn't about emptying the mind, it's about observation of the thoughts that are there, like watching clouds drift across a deep blue sky or observing buses travelling down an empty road (at which point you know you must be meditating!). The difference is, you choose not to be pulled down by the thoughts by not giving them any emotional charge. It really is liberating once the penny drops that you are not your thoughts.

There are hundreds of ways to meditate. The simplest is Breath Meditation, which involves sitting quietly observing the breath entering and leaving the body. Then there's Walking Meditation, which is simply observing yourself walking, mindful only of what you're physically doing. Watching the flickering flames of a candle is meditation, as is being absorbed utterly in a hobby. There is even a type of meditation where you concentrate fully on doing the household chores, totally engaged in what you're doing.

Idea 49 - Space invaders

To be honest, the easiest way to get into meditation is to throw out all those books and replace them with CDs. There's no way you can read the instructions whilst attempting to meditate, you'll just get distracted, which defeats the whole point of the meditation experience. So, which method to go for? Go for the relaxation ones to start with. You might not think of these as meditation, but anything that helps concentrate the mind fully *is* meditation. Recording your own meditation tape works well too, although you might think this is a bit naff.

Try another idea... Now that you're working on your mind space, check out **IDEA 48, *Breathe in, breathe out!***

Body Scan Meditation is also a great one to start with. The first time you do this, tape a script so that next time you can just listen with headphones. Find a comfortable space and lie down, allowing your eyes to gently close. Be aware of your breathing in and out. When you're ready, bring your attention to your left foot and the toes on your foot. Feel like you're breathing into your foot (sounds weird I know). On your script say something like, 'I feel my foot, my foot is relaxed, my foot is completely relaxed.' Work your way up your legs, up through your body and into your head. Don't leave anything out, including the naughty bits! Spend two or three minutes at the end just lying on your back in silence, then bring yourself back to the room. Nice and gently does it. It isn't advisable at this point to dip into the BBC's sound archive and use a klaxon or the Titanic's foghorn, as this will

Defining idea... **'Life is what happens to you while you're busy making other plans.'**
JOHN LENNON, trying to tell us to be here and now not here and there.

215

undoubtedly undo that nice relaxed, warm, cuddly feeling. The whole thing should last about 20 minutes or so and practising once a day should really make a difference. And what differences should you expect? Striving for a result is a real no-no in meditation, but between you, me and the gatepost, you should definitely start seeing the world through those rose-coloured specs.

How did it go?

Q I started quite well and then I fell asleep. What can I do to stay awake?

A Try sitting up instead of lying down. You don't have to do the whole cross-legged-on-the-floor thing (if you do, make sure your back doesn't sag), just sit in an upright chair, with your feet firmly on the ground and your back as straight as you can make it. It will be more difficult to nod off this way.

Q I keep forgetting to practise. How can I remember?

A Don't give yourself a hard time about it, just practise whenever you remember to. Make an appointment with yourself in your diary and stick to it.

50
Look on the bright side

It's time to reach for those rose-coloured spectacles...

It's easy to wake up every morning cheesed off with life, as once you're in the habit of thinking negatively it can be hard to see the good stuff that makes life worth living.

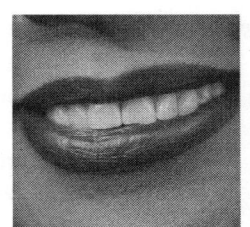

Before getting your prescription for magic see-life-differently glasses, it's important to understand that this isn't about conning yourself that things are better than they are. It's about learning to appreciate the good things that are already coming your way. I know this might not be what you feel like doing right now. You might be in a really bad way. However, even when our lives are really in the gutter we generally have something to be grateful for, even if it's just the fact that we're tough enough to have made it this far.

It's really hard to turn your life around and realise that sometimes it's only your perception of situations that make them bad or good. Changing that perception and switching from gloom mode to upbeat observation is sadly not as easy as simply

Here's an idea for you...

Try changing your attitude to a positive one for 20 days. If you catch yourself being a misery guts then you have to start again from day one. Watch your language and notice what you say about yourself and other people. How do you respond when someone asks you how you are? Do you say, 'Fantastic'? Or do you say, 'Not bad'? Do you get pulled into office gossip and find yourself being less than charitable to Linda on reception or the guy with bad breath in accounts? Remember, if you're indulging in bad-mouthing them, what could they be saying about you?

'bucking up'. It takes a gradual shift in attitude and, like so many big jobs, it starts with small steps. Here's a great technique to help tweak your take on life. It's called the 'Bedtime Threes'.

Right. Get a nice little notebook, not a scabby cheap one. Splash out on one that really feels important. Then, every night, just before you turn the light out, write down three good things that happened that day. These could be small things or big things. I have down in my notebook a time when someone stopped me from falling over on the bus and a time when I found some change on the ground. I write down who I'm grateful to every day. Sometimes it's my husband and other times it might be my mum or other family member or just somebody I randomly met on the street.

You might be feeling slightly nauseous at this point. How can a person be so goddam grateful every day? The fact is, all this gratefulness is to help *you*. It's partly a mind trick. By seeing the small good things, you'll suddenly realise that life isn't all bad, whatever they tell you on the news. And that's another thing. Don't ever listen to the news just before you go to sleep. Part of the theory of the 'Bedtime Threes' is that you fill your mind with something positive rather than something

Idea 50 - **Look on the bright side**

negative so unless you come from planet Zog, news broadcasts won't tend to emphasise the great things that happened that day. By the same token, give some thought to your bedtime reading. Going to bed with an upbeat book is far better than drifting off to mentally replay *American Psycho* all night.

Perhaps you need to set up some good habits for everyday living. See IDEA 47, *Daily habits*.

Try another idea...

Another trick to get those magic glasses sparkling is to try to see the beauty in everything, even in the ugly things around you. Even if you live in a town. Especially if you live in a town. Find a park, look for a bird, try to see the sky, go to the river if you have one. Watch the rain beating on the windowpane. Look up and see how architects have often added interesting architectural features on the parapets of buildings. No idea why though, perhaps to impress the seagulls. In big cities, it's easy to go to exhibitions where you can find beauty in art or to concerts to find beauty in music. And you don't necessarily need to spend a fortune, as many cities have free events (scout for these in local newspapers).

When you're tempted to get out those miserable, dark, satanic, moaning glasses again, ask yourself how your attitude is serving you. The only person you really affect with your Eeyore groaning is yourself.

'Human felicity is produced not so much by great pieces of good fortune that seldom happen as by little advantages that occur everyday.'
BENJAMIN FRANKLIN

Defining idea...

219

How did it go?

Q **This is all very well, but I'm not cut out for this positive-thinking lark. If things are bad, how can I pretend they're good?**

A *It's not about a Pollyanna world where everything smells of roses. It's about focus. If something is bad, you have two choices: change it or put up with it. If you have to put up with it, focusing on it will drive you nuts. As an old Italian boyfriend of mine would say (it's the only phrase he can say in English), 'It's a reality, so get used to it!'*

Q **My mind is such a negative misery guts. Will I ever be able to think more positively?**

A *Remember it is practice, practice, practice. And watch how you talk to yourself – stop calling yourself names not even your worst enemy would use. You mind has been able to wander around like a black grumpy cloud all its life – now it's time to show it who's in charge. Gently does it though! When you find yourself down a negative spiral, gently pull your mind back to better things. Affirmations can help. Affirmations are positive statements, designed to focus your mind. Check out Stuart Wilde's book* Affirmations *(Amazon should oblige you here).*

51
And so to bed...

It's two in the morning and you're still counting those blasted sheep. In fact, two million five hundred thousand have jumped over that gate so far!

Understanding the sleeping process is half the battle in terms of insomnia. Actually doing something about it isn't necessarily the answer. Remember, we're human beings not human doings!

Sleeping should be the easiest thing in the world and could go something like this: you get into bed, close your eyes and before you know it Big Ben is ringing in your ears and your partner has brought you a cup of tea.

When the sleep muscle fails to perform, it's torture. No amount of tossing, turning, reading, huffing and puffing will waft you off to dreamland. I had a week of it in 1991 and I swore I'd do everything I could to avoid a repeat performance.

Here's an idea for you... If you're getting to sleep OK yet still feel knackered when you wake up, you might be getting the quantity but not the quality. Do some detective work. Is your mattress all lumpy and bumpy? Invest in a really good bed and change it at least every five years. Is your room too hot? If safe, sleep with the window open. Is there noise and light that's bothering you? Try eye masks and earplugs.

The first rule is never to worry about anything when you're in bed. Will your bank be open at 2.30 a.m. in the morning? No. Can you phone your client and tell him you might be late for tomorrow's meeting? Possibly, but you won't be Mr Popular. Apparently we have over 60,000 thoughts a day, of which 80% are the same thoughts! So, not only do we worry incessantly, but we worry about the same thing repeatedly.

These repetitive thoughts are stress triggers. You may think that you're just worrying about the bank manager, but your body thinks that the sabre-toothed tiger is about to eat you alive. It therefore releases adrenaline, which raises the heart rate and encourages the release of glucose from storage. With your heart going like the clappers, it's unlikely you'll be able to drift off to sleep. In fact, if you had a club and a fur loincloth you'd be hunting for woolly mammoths right now! Getting to the bottom of what might be bothering you isn't an option in the middle of the night. However, relaxation CDs are great for switching off the mind and a company called Innertalk (www.innertalk.co.uk) do a fantastic CD entitled *Sleep Soundly*.

Adrenaline can also be pumped round the body for a different reason: food intolerances. If you have an undiagnosed intolerance to, say, wheat products, each time you eat something with wheat in it, in comes the adrenaline. The best way to identify these intolerances is to consult a fully qualified nutritionist.

*Idea 51 – **And so to bed...***

Cortisol, another stress hormone, increases glucose production in the body, which in turn increases blood sugar levels making you feel wide awake and ready for action. Your brain is the single biggest user of glucose. Even whilst you're asleep your brain is steering the ship, so to speak. If glucose levels drop, then it's thought that adrenaline and cortisol stimulate the release of stored glucose. And guess what else those two hormones do? They get your old ticker pumping away again so you wake up with a thumping heart that feels like a wild horse has dragged you through a hedge backwards. As alcohol is a simple sugar, which raises blood sugar levels quickly, the sharp drop that follows wakes you up.

Try another idea...

See IDEA 49, ***Space invaders***, for a detailed description of the Body Scan Meditation. There's more about blood sugar in IDEA 3, ***Vital energy***, and check out IDEA 48, ***Breathe in, breathe out!***, for an Eastern approach to calming the mind.

Try this sleep prescription. Get to bed at roughly the same time each evening so that your body gets the message that this is the routine. Just before bed have a warm bath or a hot drink (not a big cup otherwise you'll be up in the night for a different reason). I like camomile tea or alternatively Celestial Seasonings do 'Sleepytime' tea. Eat a little snack before going to bed to stop your blood sugar dropping in the night. Choose a bite-sized snack that contains a little bit of protein to help slow down the release of sugar, such as cottage cheese on an oatcake with a couple of slices of apple. Don't do your workout at the gym late at night as it gets your heart pumping. And watch your caffeine intake too, as it can decrease your night-time levels of the sleep hormone melatonin and stay in your

Defining idea...

'To sleep: perchance to dream.'
WILLIAM SHAKESPEARE, who must surely have burned the midnight oil!

223

Defining idea...

'And so to bed.'
SAMUEL PEPYS, who must have slept like a hedgehog in hibernation after all his energetic extracurricular activity

body for at least 15 hours. Plan your work so that you do the taxing stuff in the morning when you're at your peak – getting into bed wired isn't a recipe for kip. Once in bed, try a Body Scan Meditation, relaxing each muscle in your body in turn and breathing deeply into your abdomen as you go. Make sure the room is dark enough, but make sure you get enough light during the rest of the day, which is essential for good sleep hormone function. You might consider a light box to boost your quota (www.healthy-house.co.uk). Lastly, getting an hour's sleep in before midnight is worth two hours after midnight. This really isn't an old wives' tale, as our bodies work in a cycle called the circadian rhythm where at each particular hour our bodies are being regenerated and repaired. Our organs obviously work well at other times too, but we do need sleep to regenerate. The liver, gallbladder and lungs are at their optimum whilst we're asleep.

Sweet dreams!

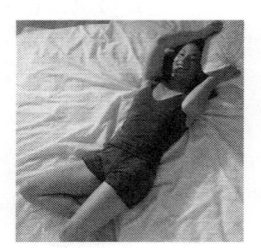

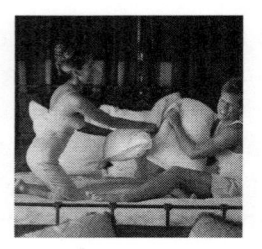

Idea 51 – **And so to bed...**

Q I tried the Body Scan Meditation and I couldn't concentrate. Is that normal?

How did it go?

A *Don't worry. No one can concentrate straight off. Persist, but if you find yourself getting frustrated, get up and go and listen to some relaxing music. Take your duvet and a hot water bottle if you think you might be cold. Don't worry about not sleeping. It will pass.*

Q I really miss my evening work-out. What are the alternatives?

A *Try doing yoga, Pilates or gentle martial arts. These will slow you down rather than speed you up. We all need a balance of aggressive (male) energy like the gym and softer (female) energy like stretching and breathing. Getting a tape and doing it at home is possible but classes encourage you to keep up the habit and remain disciplined.*

Q I can't get to sleep, but then I can't get up in the morning either. Why's that?

A *It sounds like your adrenaline cycle is out, meaning that you've got your foot jammed down on the accelerator peddle of life, which doesn't leave you with enough 'gas' (adrenaline) to get you out of bed the following day. Look at changing your lifestyle and, as a last point, if you're depressed consider a trip to your GP.*

52 Brilliant Ideas – **Get healthy for good**

52
Retreat!

You've had enough! Life, work and the universe in general have become too much. You're having a 'Stop the world I want to get off' moment.

A retreat can be a great way to relax and unwind. The pressure is off and you can concentrate on relaxing! Regeneration and relaxation are incredibly important to health.

Health is about balance. Yes there's the doing (exercise, eating right, etc), but the other side of the coin is the being. Just as the day is for activity and the night is for rest, we need regeneration to get the required balance for a healthy mind and body.

Retreats are all about putting your wellbeing first for a while rather than it being an afterthought in an otherwise hectic schedule. Since you're the most important person in the world and your importance to others is radically reduced if you're not 'good within your own skin', don't see this as a purely selfish thing. It's for the benefit of friends and family too. If I had a few months to spare, I wouldn't mind checking out the following:

Here's an idea for you...

You don't have to go all the way to Thailand to retreat. Look at doing a spa day locally (try www.aveda.com or www.elemis.com). Even just going for a massage or a facial can give you that spa feeling. Also, you could always learn massage at home – look at www.nealsyardremedies.com for wonderful oils to practice with.

www.glutenfreeholidays.com
This is a very comprehensive site, with information on gluten-free package holidays in Europe and independent holidays in the rest of the world. There's also plenty of worldwide information and links listed by an A-Z of countries. There's even a list of airlines that offer gluten-free meals.

www.healthoasisresort.com
For those who prefer a beachfront resort, the Health Oasis Resort could be just the ticket. Based in Koh Samui, Thailand, their programmes are designed to promote self-healing in the body and include cleansing, fasting, pampering, colonics, classes and lectures. You get to choose exactly what appeals to you. Programmes run from three hours to three weeks and they even offer training courses and, for the smaller folk, the Healing Child Center.

www.resortstowellness.com
A comprehensive site that's more like a directory. It lists spas by location (Asia, Canada, Europe, Latin America and the USA) and by spa types (e.g. lifestyle or cityscape). The focus here is really on the individual and they have a very informative section on Executive Health.

www.ayurveda.org

If five-star luxury is your thing, this isn't the resort for you. Set in the Indian Countryside in a place called Coonoor, this retreat offers detox, anti-aging and stress packages amongst many many others. They use traditional Ayurvedic methods combined with yoga and meditation and even offer a Total Renewal package for 30–75 year olds. They also have training for those who are interested in becoming yoga teachers.

www.hippocratesinst.org

In the lush vegetation and sunshine of Florida, this resort offers an impressive range of programmes, including Lifechange, which focuses on education about nutrition and lifestyle choices and the maintenance of wellness. They also use Nutripuncture, a method of acupuncture without needles that harmonises the body's energy flow. There is a choice of accommodation and the choice of pools (sea salt, cold plunge and recreational).

www.tenthousandwaves.com

Based in New Mexico, this spa takes it's principal from Japan and this theme runs through the treatments and the minimal but elegant lodging. Ten Thousand Waves is primarily a day spa, but there is nearby accommodation with a good choice of amenities.

Try another idea...

IDEA 34, *Home spa*, will give you some ideas if time and budget are an issue.

Defining idea...

'Health is wealth.'
Buddist saying

www.aspatolife.com
A guide to spas throughout Europe and Barbados. There is an extensive list of treatments, many water-based and all with the emphasis on restoring balance to the body and promoting body-awareness.

www.templespa.ie
An Irish country house on the site of an ancient monastery, the focus here really is on relaxation and wellbeing, with a choice of massages, hot stone therapy and reflexology. There is the choice of weekend and midweek stays and a range of packages, including one designed for mums-to-be.

www.sanoviv.com
A medical institute that deals with chronic illnesses such as lupus, Parkinson's disease, cancer and multiple sclerosis. It also caters for those who are interested in detox and cleansing programmes. Sanoviv offers a complete health assessment and will tailor programmes to your specific needs. They use diagnostic testing, botanical therapies and a wide range of medical treatments and protocols.

Idea 52 – **Retreat!**

Q **How can I carve out the time to go on a retreat?**

A Why not treat the time spent on a retreat as a priority as opposed to a waste of time. Book retreat time in as holiday and write it in your diary. Sometimes you'll find that although it looks like a lot of money to go on a retreat, it works out cheaper because everything is included.

Q **How do I know what type of retreat to choose?**

A Use your instinct, but be careful. If you're a stress junky you'll be tempted to go for places that offer loads of activities. That's fine, but are you attracted to it because you'll be doing more doing? Look at your needs. Are you stressed, ill or just in need of pampering? It's also helpful if you choose somewhere on the recommendation of a friend so that you know what to expect, otherwise just go with an open mind and enjoy the experience.

How did it go?

Bonus ideas

52 Brilliant Ideas – **Get healthy for good**

1
Have a holiday at your desk

Imbue the old nine-to-five with a certain glamour and you'll be amazed at how much tension seeps out of your life.

You'll be raising your standards and that means lowering your stress levels.

Forty years has taught me that there are two ways to have a perfect day. One is in the grand tradition of the Lou Reed song. You hang out for a whole day with someone you really, really love who is loving you right back – or at least tolerating you. You don't have to do anything because just being with the beloved is so blissful it blocks out the boring little problems that usually stress you out. If you manage twenty days like this in your whole life time, you're doing pretty well.

And then there's the second way. You build a perfect day for yourself and by adding grace and glamour to your life, you remove stress. It takes a little thought. But it is more reliable than true love. You can have a holiday of the 'mind' on even the most mundane day.

REBOOT YOUR COMMUTE

Give your journey to work an overhaul. Set yourself targets. Instead of a drag, see it as a purposeful part of your day. If it involves walking, buy a pedometer. Learn a language. Use the time to repeat your mantras for the day. Be creative: write a page

Here's an idea for you... Clothes can play a huge part in improving the quality of our life. Every morning choose one thing that makes your heart sing – a colour you love, a fabric that embraces you, a piece of jewellery with sentimental attachment. Next time you're shopping buy clothes that help you radiate confidence.

of free-hand prose on the journey in (not if you drive of course!). Start working up the characters for your novel. It's a terrific time to practice mindfulness, which can deliver the benefits of meditation. The list is endless.

BOOST YOUR ENVIRONMENT

Your starter question: what five changes would make your work environment more pleasant. Here's mine. Getting rid of piles of papers and magazines that need to be filed. Investing in a china cup and no more sharing the office's grubby, chipped ones. Cheering up my desk with a bunch of pink tulips. Cleaning my keyboard – so filthy it's a health hazard. Turning down the ringtone volume on my phone. Everyday find some way to make your surroundings more pleasant.

BEAT THE MID-AFTERNOON SLUMP

When you feel the slump kicking in, stop working and get away from your workstation if you can. Go for a short walk in the sunshine, or take a nap. If you can't, try this: palm your eyes in your hand for a few minutes and visualise a calm and beautiful place. See this in as much detail as possible.

Bonus Idea 1 – **Have a holiday at your desk**

THE JOURNEY HOME

This needs a different mood from the journey to work. If you listen to music, make it different from the tunes you play in the morning – slower, deeper. Small stuff like that really helps to emphasise that this is your transition period. Have a project that you work on at this time (planning your holiday is good). And if you read, keep the tone light. If in the morning you read French verbs or the novels of Dostoyevsky, read P.G. Wodehouse on the way home.

Defining idea...

> *'You can make more friends in two months by becoming interested in other people than you can in two years by trying to get other people interested in you.'*
> DALE CARNEGIE, founding father of the self-help movement

SPREAD LOVE

When you pass someone in distress send them 'serenity' or 'calm' as a thought. Spread good and happy thoughts wherever you go. Smile. Be gracious. Be kind, compassionate, a force for good.

Not every day can be a high day or holiday, but changing your mindset, looking for grace and sheer fun in previous black holes of misery turns you into a force for light and transforms your day-to-day grind – it's the art of living lightly and it gets easier the more you look for opportunities to practise your skill.

How did it go?

Q **This may work for some people but my environment is so depressing, it gets me down. How can I get a lift?**

A *Try this: repeat to yourself 'Beauty before me. Beauty behind me. Beauty above me. Beauty below me.' With each direction look very hard for what is beautiful before you, behind, you, etc., etc. Search for a source of gratification. Do this anywhere, anytime – stuck in traffic, loading the dishwasher, waiting for the bus – and you will be quite amazed at how often you find a source of beauty and wonder in your vicinity – usually you'll find four. This game also takes a bit of concentration and lifts the spirits, I find. It helps you get out of your normal way of thinking, which makes you more creative.*

Q **I have tried your ideas but still feel stressed at work and feel terrible mid-afternoon. Am I missing a trick?**

A *One workplace in eight is as dry as the Sahara. Yes, rehydration is important but turn getting your litre and a half of water into an event. Keep ice at hand, or a twist of lemon. Sip your drinks from a straw. Or choose a different fruit juice every week and have a glass of juice cut with fizzy water. Sure it's a faff. That's the point. Make the everyday special. You could also try my father-in-law's tip that put an end to his mid-afternoon headaches. Stop. Slowly peel an orange. Relish it. (I'd add: use a napkin and a plate – a sticky keyboard won't help your stress levels!) Really taste that orange. As a general rule, if you do eat at your desk, make as big a deal as you can of it.*

This idea originally appeared in *Stress proof your life: 52 brilliant ideas for taking control*, by Elisabeth Wilson. Turn to page 254 for a special offer on this book.

2

Don't do that, do this

The thought of cold turkey ruffles you. Nicotine patches don't cover it. And gum just won't stick. Why not look at some of the alternative methods that may be all you need to quit while you're ahead (and still alive)?

You may feel that so-called 'new age' treatments are not for you. Most of the treatments available, however, have been around for aeons — far longer than cigarettes — and are founded on ancient wisdoms.

Ask around and see if any of your friends have tried any alternative methods. For some people they're the perfect answer. Treatment can sometimes be pricey, but if you give up smoking you'll make your money back in no time.

QUICK FIXES

Never thought you'd be sticking a needle in yourself to stop being a drug addict? Acupuncture has the painless answer. Tackle the addiction, relieve stress, improve your sleep patterns. Those needles have a point.

Acupuncture works on a pattern of energy lines running through the body which have key points, like junctions in a power system. Tap into these and you can

Here's an idea for you... **Join a gym or take up a regular exercise routine. Working your body triggers the release of endorphins into your bloodstream, which creates a natural high.**

change the flow of energy. Its a system of medicine that's used in a whole range of conditions. In some parts of the world it's even used as a substitute for anaesthetics in surgery. And it works.

In treating smoking, acupuncture works on the principle that changing the energy flow can provide valuable assistance in reducing both your craving and the tensions that come with giving up. It's not at all painful, despite how it looks. Acupuncture is widely used in helping heroin users get off the drug.

The secret is to choose the right practitioner, and the best bet here is to go by recommendation. If all else fails, look for a complementary or alternative medicine centre near you.

LOOK INTO MY EYES

Sneak up on your habit and tackle it while it's not looking with hypnosis. Talking to your subconscious could help root out the underlying causes of your addiction and give you hidden support.

Hypnosis is absolutely harmless and relaxes you to a point somewhere between being asleep and awake, rather like how you feel as you are just drifting off to sleep. Once you are in this state, your mind is open to suggestion, and a skilled hypnotist will plant subtle counter-triggers in your mind to ward off your desire for cigarettes. It can also help to generally relax you and bring down your stress levels.

Defining idea... **'More doctors smoke camels than any other cigarette!'**
R.J. Reynolds Industries advertising slogan, 1946

Once again, the knack is finding the right practitioner for you.

YOU CAN DO IT STANDING ON YOUR HEAD

Yoga in itself is not a direct method for giving up smoking, but it can prove to be a very useful ally. It's not a 'go-for-the-burn' physical activity and certain forms of it (Iyengar yoga is a good example) are very gentle indeed; you simply go with what you feel is comfortable.

What yoga can offer is a method of increasing the flow of endorphins through the body (the so-called 'natural happy drug'), creating a deep sense of well-being, which is both relaxing and energising. It's rather like creating a still pool in your life, and once you have learned a few positions it can be practised any time. Many leisure centres have yoga classes.

Similar claims could be made for meditation, which focuses on breathing. It's a great alternative to a smoke and gives you a natural high. Both yoga and meditation are relatively low cost options.

TAKE YOUR PICK

It's worth sampling a range of these alternative therapies and seeing what kind of mix works for you. From crystal healing to Bach Flower Remedies, from herbal remedies to primal scream, there could just be the method out there that will help you give up cigarettes. So check out your nearest complementary medicine centre, or even ask your doctor for what's available in your neighbourhood.

> *Defining idea...*
>
> 'More than 34 million working days are lost each year because of smoking-related sick leave.'
> www.patient.co.uk

How did it go?

Q All this new age stuff is just a pile of dingo's kidneys. It doesn't really work, does it?

A Don't knock it till you've tried it. When steam locomotives were first invented some people said that travelling at more than 25 mph would be fatal, that people's brains would explode. Ask drivers on any main road at rush hour and they'll tell you the opposite – it's travelling under that speed that's the problem. There's progress for you. Seriously, there's tens of thousands of people for whom these therapies have worked – you've just got to find the right one for you.

Q Why should I pay my hard-earned cash on a half chance that something might work when I can't afford it?

A You've no problem dishing out for a pack of your favourite drug though, have you? And that's guaranteed to kill you in the end. If you can't afford expensive therapists, check out your local library for a book on the subject. Most local authorities will also have information about very cheap courses – again, your local library is the best place to ask.

Q Would smoking herbal cigarettes be a good alternative?

A It really depends on whether you like smoking the equivalent of a garden hedge or not. You don't get the nicotine hit of a cigarette, just the sensation of setting fire to a bunch of leaves and sucking it into your lungs. Not recommended for most of us, but do try it out and let us know how you get on.

This idea originally appeared in *Stop smoking: 52 brilliant ideas to kick the habit for good*, by Peter Cross and Clive Hopwood. Turn to page 254 for a special offer on this book.

3
Start right

A well-balanced breakfast can have a noticeable impact on your child's health, mood, ability to concentrate – and eating habits for the rest of the day.

So, no matter how rushed you are, it's vital you make sure there's time for a nutritious family breakfast.

The first meal of the day is considered to be the most important for a number of reasons. Eating the right foods at breakfast time will stabilise blood sugar levels, making it less likely that your child will crave a boost from sugary, high fat or processed foods later in the day. Some studies have also found strong links between eating breakfast and improved learning, a better ability to concentrate, less irritability, more energy, less likelihood of overeating during the rest of the day and a general feeling of well-being. The foods to avoid at breakfast most of the time are the sugary and over processed ones. They may go down well with your child, but sugary foods tend to lead to cravings for yet more sugary, over processed foods by midmorning. So avoid foods like chocolate- or honey-coated and sugar-frosted cereals – or those that have been baked into clusters. Chocolate spread, croissants, muffins, breakfast and cereal bars and pastries are also all best left off the menu. Instead, try to ensure your child has a combination of slow-releasing carbohydrates and protein, which will help to keep him full and offer a steady supply of energy until lunchtime. In addition, aim to add a fruit or vegetable to the meal. Read through the following suggestions for inspiration:

- A *wholegrain cereal* (with minimal added sugar and fat – compare labels to find the best) served with chopped banana and semi-skimmed milk (NB semiskimmed milk should only be given to children of two and over, younger children should have full fat milk).

    A recent study at Harvard Medical School showed that people who eat wholegrain cereals every morning are less likely to be obese than those who skip breakfast altogether. In addition, they are half as likely to have blood sugar problems which can lead to type 2 diabetes to have high cholesterol – both are risk factors for heart disease.

- *Unsweetened porridge* – do try the plain, 'instant' microwave version for speed – made with half semi-skimmed milk and half water. Don't be tempted to add sugar or honey to sweeten it – use finely chopped fresh or dried fruit such as chopped strawberries or raisins instead. Porridge has a low GI (glycaemic index) score which means it gives a slow, sustained release of energy – helping you to feel fuller for longer. Oats have also been shown to help lower blood cholesterol levels.

Here's an idea for you...

For older children, try a bacon sandwich. A study carried out at Reading University found that a bacon sandwich breakfast was one of the best for improving brain power. Choose unsmoked, lean bacon and trim away fatty rind before grilling or dry frying. Serve between wholegrain, granary or seeded bread with the very thinnest smear of butter or spread.

- *Wholegrain, multigrain, seeded or fruit toast* with low sugar peanut or other nut butter, reduced sugar jam, a thin spread of butter and Marmite (use Marmite sparingly as it is high in salt), mashed banana, cream cheese or ham slices. Serve with some fruit juice or fruit slices on the side.

  > **Defining idea...**
  >
  > *'Our results suggest that breakfast may really be the most important meal of the day.'*
  >
  > DR MARK PEREIRA, research scientist at Harvard Medical School

  The breads recommended above are the best breakfast choice as they release energy more slowly than white bread. White is fine too, as long as you don't offer it every day.

- *Eggs* – scrambled, poached or boiled served with a toasted wholegrain muffin and cherry tomatoes. Using Omega 3-rich eggs, which are widely available from supermarkets, is a great way to boost your child's intake of this useful essential fatty acid. Important for a healthy heart and circulation – Omega 3 is also thought to help improve children's concentration and calm hyperactivity.

- *A pot of natural bio-yogurt with fruit and muesli stirred in.* If you add your own 'sweeteners' and other ingredients to natural yogurt, you know exactly what your child is getting. Tempt reluctant kids to eat by letting them choose their own additions and stir them in.

- A *slice of wholegrain toast* with low sugar, low salt baked beans and a glass of mixed apple and carrot juice.

  Baked beans can be counted as one of your child's five recommended daily portions of fruit and vegetables. Buying the low sugar, low salt variety really is worth the swap, as the ordinary versions can contain substantial levels of both ingredients.

How did it go?

Q **Your suggestions sound great – in theory. However, no matter how hard I try, I can never get my daughter to eat breakfast before she goes to nursery. I end up giving her biscuits to eat in the car on the way there. What do you suggest?**

A   Is the morning a bit of a rush for you?

Q **Yes ... why do you ask?**

A   When it comes to young children and eating – and this can apply equally to teenagers – one of the most important ingredients is time. Get your daughter up at least an hour before you need to leave the house, so that she has 20 minutes or so to 'come round' before you serve breakfast. (Make sure you've found her clothes, bag etc. the night before – so you're not rushed and stressed.) Then sit her at the table so she can't be distracted, and serve her something really small – a large plate of food can be really off-putting first thing. I find a piece of toast cut into a couple of animal shapes with cookie or play dough cutters always goes down well, or a small tub of flavoured fromage frais. I always add a favourite chopped fruit on the side – and a drink, of course. Whilst doing this, I would also make sure that you let her know that you've run out of biscuits.

This idea originally appeared in *Healthy cooking for children: 52 brilliant ideas to dump the junk*, by Mandy Francis. Turn to page 254 for a special offer on this book.

Brilliant resources

Personal trainer at home
www.exerciseregister.com
www.privatetraining.com

Home gym
www.exercisebands.com
www.newitts.com
www.simplefitnesssolutions.com

Home cleaners
www.mollymaid.com (US)
www.themovechannel.com

Garden services
www.clifton.co.uk
www.improvenet.com (US)
www.servicemagic.com (US)
www.thegardenco.co.uk

Get organised
www.allmy.co.uk – is a software package for all your vital documents and reminders – e.g. birthdays
www.myorganisedlife.com – organise the five core areas of your life (self, finance, home, family, work)
www.needmoretime.co.uk – virtual office
www.quintessentially.com – can help organise holidays, restaurants and theatre bookings, club memberships, car rentals, lifestyle advisors

52 Brilliant Ideas – **Get healthy for good**

How did it go?

Let someone else run around
www.beckandcall.co.uk – they do the chores
www.courture.co.uk – upmarket privileges
www.prioritytraveller.com
www.tenuk.com – Concierge and Services

Let someone else cook
www.nutrifileonline.com
www.purepackage.co.uk – healthy eating for those short on time

Laundry services
www.allironedout.co.uk – get the washing and ironing done for you
www.citidex.com/516.htm (US)
www.thebiglaundry.com

Online food shopping
www.foodferry.com
www.ocado.com
www.organicdelivery.com
www.safeway.com
www.sainsburystoyou.co.uk
www.shamra.com (US)
www.tesco.com

Find a nutritionist
www.bant.org.uk

The end...

Or is it a new beginning?

We hope that the ideas in this book will have inspired you to try some new things. You should be well on your way to a healthier, fitter, more fulfilled and balanced you, brimming with good intentions.

You're mean, you're motivated and you don't care who knows it.

So why not let *us* know all about it? Tell us how you got on. What did it for you – what helped you beat the demons that were holding you back? Maybe you've got some tips of your own you want to share (see next page if so). And if you liked this book you may find we have even more brilliant ideas that could change other areas of your life for the better.

You'll find the Infinite Ideas crew waiting for you online at www.infideas.com.

Or if you prefer to write, then send your letters to:
Get healthy for good
The Infinite Ideas Company Ltd
36 St Giles, Oxford, OX1 3LD, United Kingdom

We want to know what you think, because we're all working on making our lives better too. Give us your feedback and you could win a copy of another *52 Brilliant Ideas* book of your choice. Or maybe get a crack at writing your own.

Good luck. Be brilliant.

Offer one

CASH IN YOUR IDEAS

We hope you enjoy this book. We hope it inspires, amuses, educates and entertains you. But we don't assume that you're a novice, or that this is the first book that you've bought on the subject. You've got ideas of your own. Maybe our author has missed an idea that you use successfully. If so, why not send it to yourauthormissedatrick@infideas.com, and if we like it we'll post it on our bulletin board. Better still, if your idea makes it into print we'll send you four books of your choice or the cash equivalent. You'll be fully credited so that everyone knows you've had another Brilliant Idea.

Offer two

HOW COULD YOU REFUSE?

Amazing discounts on bulk quantities of Infinite Ideas books are available to corporations, professional associations and other organisations.

For details call us on:
+44 (0)1865 514888
fax: +44 (0)1865 514777
or e-mail: info@infideas.com

Where it's at...

Adams, Williams, 157
Aesop, 133
ageing gracefully, 81-84
alcohol, 2, 9, 20, 49, 55, 57-58, 141, 156, 223
Alexander Technique, 122
Allen, Woody, 91
aloe vera, 8
amyloglucosidase, 5
anaphylactic shock, 53
antioxidants, 21-22, 41-42, 58, 82, 155
Aristophenes, 119
Aristotle, 205
Atkins diet, 88
automatic pilot, living on, 195

B vitamins, 20, 42
    see also vitamins
bacteria, 3, 4, 9, 48-49
Baker, Sydney, 3
Barkley, Charles, 115
basics of good nutrition, 85-88
bathtime, 127-128
Baudelaire, Charles, 87
beetroot, 2, 7, 30, 58
betacarotene, 30, 82
better sex, 1-256
Bhagavad Gita, 141
biotin, 20
bloated, 54
blood sugar, 10-13, 18-19, 20, 36, 39, 64-66, 78, 223
bowel, 3, 7-8, 37
brain, 19, 22, 31, 35, 52, 73, 87, 168, 181-182, 197, 223
breakfast, 12, 14, 44, 54, 64, 78-80, 107, 147

breathing, 53, 58, 65, 90, 121, 139, 140-141, 209, 210, 212, 215, 224-225

calcium, 22-23, 30
camomile (the tea that thinks it's a lawn), 150, 223
Carnegie, Dale, 197, 200, 201
Carson, Rachel, 61
changing your attitude, 218
Charles, Prince, 27
chewing, 1
    see also breathing, walking
children, encouraging good habits in, 151-154
chocolate, 14, 20, 52, 57, 63, 66, 73, 106, 119, 141
cholesterol, 3, 29, 33-35, 78
choosing what to eat, 77
clutter, 173-176, 205
coaching, 187-190
Coleridge, Samuel Taylor, 49
Colgan, Michael, 106
confidence, 166
couch potatoes, 151
Covey, Stephen R., 201, 205
cycling, 83, 135-138

dairy products, 40, 52, 57-58, 68
dancing, 96
decluttering, 175
definite in your purpose, 166
delegating responsibilities, 125
Demar, Clarence, 97
designing a new life for yourself, 169
detox, 3, 9, 31, 53, 55-58, 149, 157, 229, 230

diets, 63, 85, 88, 113
digestion, 1-5, 7-8, 10, 31, 65, 121
digestive system, 1-2, 5, 7, 9, 79, 210
Disraeli, Benjamin, 23
Dr Atkins New Diet Revolution, 88
    see also diets
Dragon Breath, 99
    see also Atkins diet
dressing for success, 161-164
drinking enough water, 47
Dwight, John Sullivan, 127

EFAs, see essential fatty acids
eggs, 14, 22, 27, 52-54, 64, 86
Einstein, Albert, 175, 183
energy, 9, 11-13, 15, 18-20, 31, 39, 50, 55-56, 64-65, 80, 86, 88, 106-107, 135-136, 173, 194, 196, 223, 225, 229
enzymes, 1, 2, 5, 22, 31-32, 82, 86
Erasmus, Udo, 35
essential fatty acids (EFAs), 34-36, 40, 43, 87, 156
exercise, exercising, 58, 65, 76, 84, 89, 90-92, 95-99, 105, 107, 110, 113, 115-116, 123-124, 128, 135-136, 139, 141, 145, 152-153, 171, 182, 203-204, 227
exfoliate, 157-158

fat, 3-4, 9, 13, 19-20, 27, 33-35, 43, 63, 65, 68, 70, 77-78, 87-88, 97, 105, 107, 135, 178, 204
fibre, 3-5, 8, 65, 86
    see also stools
finding your essence, 188
fish oils, 84

251

fish, 14, 19, 24, 26–27, 34–36, 40, 43, 49, 60–61, 64, 82, 84, 87–88, 90, 140–141, 154, 156, 188
flax seeds, 8, 58, 79
folic acid, 20
food additives, 61, 67, 69
food allergies/intolerances 19, 51, 53
Food Combining Bible, The, 2, 10
food combining, 2, 10
food diary, 52
food intolerances, 2, 54, 222
food labelling, 67–70
Franklin, Benjamin, 219
fruit, 2, 4, 8, 14, 18, 24, 25–28, 30–31, 32, 38–42, 44, 56, 58–60, 64, 66, 68, 70, 79, 82–83, 85, 141, 152–153, 155, 157
    see also vegetables
Fuller, Thomas, 31

games, 143–145, 151
Garbo, Greta, 193
getting your nutritional act together, 73–76
GI, *see* glycaemic index
ginger, 24, 30, 163
glucoamylase, 5
glucosides, 5
gluten, 52, 228
glycaemic index (GI), 12, 14, 18
goals, 90, 103, 166–168, 170–171
good nutrition, basics of, 85–88
grains, 8, 21–22, 24, 57, 65–66, 78, 85–86, 141
gym, 89–91, 101, 103, 105–107, 111, 113–116, 119, 124, 126–127, 139–140, 143, 149, 182, 193, 223, 225, 232

habits, 3, 75–76, 122, 126, 152, 203–207, 219
Healthy Kitchen, The, 79

heart rate monitor, 95–97, 105, 116, 137
Hill, Napoleon, 167
hormones, 3, 11, 13, 18–19, 26, 35, 65, 86, 128, 210, 223–224
How to Stop Worrying and Start Living, 197, 200, 201

IBS, *see* irritable bowel syndrome
insomnia, 221
insulin, 11–13, 18, 65
irritable bowel syndrome (IBS), 37, 40

juicer, 31–32, 56
juicing, 29, 31, 32
junk food, 9, 67, 77, 85, 152

Kennedy, John F., 65

Lawrence, Felicity, 69
Lennon, John, 215
liver, 2–3, 12, 22, 56, 83, 156, 224
living today, 196
looking on the bright side, 217–220
losing weight, 64
Lucretius, 53

Maffetone Method, The, 96
magnesium, 23, 30, 40, 150
Mandela, Nelson, 189
man-made chemicals, 59–62
meditate, meditation, 212–216, 229
melatonin, 223
Mies van der Rohe, Ludwig, 163
minerals, 9, 21–24, 32, 41–42, 48–49, 56, 82
multivitamins, 23–24, 39–40

Nurmi, Paavo, 96
nutritionist, 2, 5, 19, 23, 39–40, 52, 54, 64, 106, 126, 128, 222, 233
nuts, 14, 18–19, 34–35, 40, 44, 54, 64, 70, 74, 79, 82, 87, 119, 153, 156, 198, 220

omega-3, omega-6 fats, 19
Optimum Nutrition Bible, The, 22, 51, 126
organic, food, 24–28, 31–32, 42–43, 56–57, 61–62, 69, 79, 86
overweight children, 151

Paddleford, Clementine, 123
parsley, 30
pectin, 29
personal trainer, 97, 104, 127
phytochemicals, 31
Pilates, 103, 122, 141, 225
PMS, *see* premenstrual syndrome
positive habits, 204
posture, 105, 121–124, 135, 141
potassium, 23, 30
premenstrual syndrome (PMS), 37, 40
Priest, Ivy Baker, 57
pulses, 8
put yourself first, 191–194

race, racing, 89, 95, 97, 100, 131–134, 137
retreat, 227–229, 231
rotation diet, 22
run, running, 19, 22, 29–30, 58, 65, 90, 92, 99, 100–101, 109, 116, 123, 131–133, 144–145, 166, 168, 193, 195, 200, 228, 233
running partner, 100

Sandburg, Carl, 167
Schwarzenegger, Governor (who'd have thought it?) Arnold, 145
seeds, 8, 14, 18–20, 22, 34–36, 40, 44, 54, 58, 64, 74, 79, 87, 156
selenium, 22, 42, 82
self-confidence, 177, 180
self-esteem, 100, 163, 177–179, 189
self-help books, 126, 199–200, 202
sensible eating programme, 77

Index

setting goals, 166, 168
sex, better, *see* better sex
Shakespeare, William, 223
shopping, 14, 58, 74, 76, 127, 233
Sivananda, 211
skin, 26, 35, 41–44, 49, 147–150, 155–158, 212, 227
sleeping, 221, 225
    see also insomnia
Slow Burn, 96
smoking, 82, 168, 204
spa, 57, 147, 149–150, 192, 228, 229
spice, 127
    see also ginger, sporty
sports, 95–96, 99, 101, 104, 106, 112, 143–145
stomach acidity, 2
stools (we're not talking the things you sit on here), 7
stress, 2, 10, 12, 13, 18–19, 40–41, 82, 100, 128, 132, 135, 139, 210–211, 213, 222–223, 229, 231
stressed, 4, 13, 17, 20, 75, 210–211, 231
stretching, 58, 84, 97, 109–112, 124, 133, 204, 225

sugar, 8–13, 18–19, 20, 27, 36, 39, 50, 64–68, 70, 77–78, 86, 223
superfoods, 24, 29–31
supplements, 2, 24

t'ai chi, 123–124
tartrazine, 70
Thoreau, Henry David, 171
Tracy, Brian, 111
tryptophan, 20
Twain, Mark, 178

vegetables, 4, 5, 8, 14, 22, 24, 25–28, 30–32, 35, 39–42, 44, 58–60, 65–66, 75, 79–80, 82–83, 88, 127, 141, 152–155
    see also fruit
vegetarian protein, 86
Venning, Ralph, 43
visualisation, 167
vitamin A, 30
vitamin B, 20, 42
vitamin B6, 20, 40
vitamin C, 20, 22, 29–30, 42, 82, 85
vitamin E, 42, 82

vitamins, 9, 20–24, 26, 30, 32, 41–42, 56, 82, 83

walking, 84, 90–91, 97, 109, 113–118, 120, 133, 145, 152, 169, 181, 184, 204, 214
water, 3–4, 7, 8–9, 22, 28, 35–36, 42, 47–48, 49–50, 57–58, 60–61, 70, 84, 100, 105, 119–120, 138, 147–148, 150, 155–158, 191, 197, 210, 225, 230
weight loss, 63
wheel of life, 169–170, 172
wind (flatus not meteorological), 5

xeno-oestrogens, 49, 60

yoga, 38, 58, 92, 103, 110, 123–124, 136, 139, 140, 142, 225, 229
yoghurt, 9, 14, 18, 20, 33, 54, 64, 70

zinc, 20, 22, 40, 42, 69

52 Brilliant Ideas – **Get healthy for good**

Get healthy for good: 52 brilliant ideas for mind and body well-being is part of the acclaimed **52 Brilliant Ideas** series. If you found this book helpful, you may want to take advantage of this special offer exclusive to all readers of *Get healthy for good*. Choose any two books from the selection below and you'll get one of them free of charge*. See overleaf for prices and details on how to place your order.

Stress proof your life
52 brilliant ideas for taking control
By Elisabeth Wilson
SEE PAGE 235 FOR A FREE SAMPLE IDEA FROM THIS BOOK

Stop smoking
52 brilliant ideas to kick the habit for good
By Peter Cross and Clive Hopwood
SEE PAGE 239 FOR A FREE SAMPLE IDEA FROM THIS BOOK

Healthy cooking for children
52 brilliant ideas to dump the junk
By Mandy Francis
SEE PAGE 243 FOR A FREE SAMPLE IDEA FROM THIS BOOK

Control your blood pressure
52 brilliant ideas for keeping a lid on hypertension
By Dr Rob Hicks

Downshift to the good life
Scale it down and live it up
By Lynn Huggins-Cooper

Inspired creative writing
NEW EDITION
Secrets of the master wordsmiths
By Alexander Gordon Smith

Healthy heart
Keep your heart happy
By Dr Ruth Chambers

Win at the gym
Secrets of fitness and health success
By Steve Shipside

Secrets of wine
Insider insights into the real world of wine
By Giles Kime

Transform your life
52 brilliant ideas for becoming the person you want to be
By Penny Ferguson

For more detailed information on these books and others published by Infinite Ideas please visit www.infideas.com

* Postage at £2.75 per delivery address is additional.

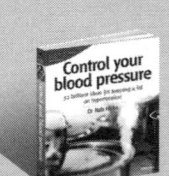

Offer

Choose any two titles from below and receive one free

Qty	Title	RRP
	Stress proof your life	£12.99
	Stop smoking	£12.99
	Healthy cooking for children	£12.99
	Control your blood pressure	£12.99
	Downshift to the good life	£12.99
	Inspired creative writing	£12.99
	Healthy heart	£12.99
	Win at the gym	£12.99
	Secrets of wine	£12.99
	Transform your life	£12.99
	Subtract lowest priced book if ordering two titles	
	Add £2.75 postage per delivery address	
	Final TOTAL	

Name: ....

Delivery address: ....

....

....

....

E-mail:..Tel (in case of problems): ....

By post Fill in all relevant details, cut out or photocopy this page and send along with a cheque made payable to Infinite Ideas. Send to: *Get healthy for good* Offer, Infinite Ideas, 36 St Giles, Oxford OX1 3LD, UK.

Credit card orders over the telephone Call +44 (0) 1865 514 888. Lines are open 9am to 5pm Monday to Friday. Just mention the promotion code 'GHFGAD07.'

Please note that no payment will be processed until your order has been dispatched. Goods are dispatched through Royal Mail within 14 working days, when in stock. We never forward personal details on to third parties or bombard you with junk mail. This offer is valid for UK and RoI residents only until 30 June 2008. Any questions or comments please contact us on 01865 514 888 or email info@infideas.com.

20% discount with The Nutrition Coach

No more calorie counting with our 'non-diet' diet – learn how to eat healthily for life

Have you spent time over the years worrying about your weight? Have you tried various diets to find that the weight comes piling on again when you start eating normally?
Are you confused by what to eat?

If so, the Nutrition Coach can help you get back on track with our very own 'Weight Loss Wonder' programme. This is no 'fad' diet – it involves busting those food myths and giving you the know-how to make sensible food choices to maximise your health and minimise your weight.

Our 12-week fully supported programme involves learning how to eat well for life. The added benefit is that you will lose weight and not regain it if you stick to the principles!

> "Throughout my twenties I felt continually unhappy with my weight but seemed unable to lose any lbs by dieting! I LOVE the rules The Nutrition Coach set out for me and have followed them successfully. All my friends and family are commenting on how well I look and with The Nutrition Coach's support I am quite sure I can continue losing weight. I feel like this is it... I can finally do it!" - **A.S., LONDON.**

The programme incorporates a 1.5 hour initial session to get you started, followed by 6 fortnightly 30-minute sessions which can be arranged over the phone if desired. You will be given small 'homeworks' along the way to keep you motivated! Email support is available in between sessions. You will be provided with:

- an information booklet covering the basics;
- monitoring sheets to track your progress;
- hand-outs after each session with the topics covered.

Topics covered include 'why diets don't work', incorporating exercise into your daily routine, eating to balance blood sugar, healthy snacking, emotional eating, food shopping, labels, junk food, the effects of alcohol and caffeine, eating out, varying your diet and more.

> "Having tried the things you suggested, I finally feel as if I'm in control of my eating, rather than the other way round. I sleep better and I don't get depression any more. It's been very simple to follow, with easy, slight changes at every step and no immediate life-altering madness." - **J.G., LONDON**

Sign up before June 2008 to benefit from 20% discount on this programme! For more details contact Kate: kate@thenutritioncoach.co.uk or book by calling 0845 0502442. Quote 'Get healthy for good' to benefit from this discount. £120 per month – discounted to £96 per month. Duration – 3 months.